**Devaluation and
Futures Markets**

Devaluation and Futures Markets

John R. Dominguez
University of California,
Los Angeles

Lexington Books
D.C. Heath and Company
Lexington, Massachusetts
Toronto   London

Copyright © 1972 by D.C. Heath and Company

All rights reserved. No part of this publication may be reproduced or transmitted in any form or by any means, electronic or mechanical, including photocopy, recording, or any information storage or retrieval system, without permission in writing from the publisher.

Published simultaneously in Canada.

Printed in the United States of America.

International Standard Book Number: 0–669–83907–8.

Library of Congress Catalog Card Number: 72–2016.

To my querida wife
        Karen Jeanne Darcy
**With my deepest love and appreciation
for her patience, understanding, and encouragement.**

Table of Contents

List of Tables	xv
List of Figures	ix
Foreword, Paul A. Samuelson	ix
Preface	xiii

Chapter 1 The Evolution and Characteristics of Futures Markets — 1

Historical Development of Futures Trading	1
Modern Futures Trading	2
Futures Trading Participants	3
Determination of Futures Prices	4
Trading Volume	5
Contractual Arrangements	6
Deferred Delivery Grades	7
Grade Price Differentials	7
Delivery Months	8
Margin Requirements	8
Cocoa: New York and London Exchanges	9

Chapter 2 The Temporal and Spatial Elements of Arbitrage — 13

Definition and Description of Arbitrage Activity	13
Arbitrage and Devaluation	14
The Arbitrage Decision	15
General Types of Arbitrage Transactions	16
Case I: Static Arbitrage under Conditions of Certainty	19
Case II: Dynamic Arbitrage under Conditions of Certainty	21
Case III: Static Arbitrage under Conditions of Uncertainty	31
Case IV: Dynamic Arbitrage under Conditions of Uncertainty	34

vii

Chapter 3	**Devaluation: Its Effect on Futures and Arbitrage Incentive**	**37**
	The Appropriate Trading Contracts	37
	Selection of the Trading Day	43
	Problems in the Representative Price	44
	New York Futures Price	44
	London Futures Price	46
	New York and London Arbitrage Incentive	46
	The Foreign Exchange Rate and Price Conversion	49
	Possible Biases in Estimating Arbitrage Incentive	50
	Impact of Devaluation Expectations on the Basis	51
	Variables Influencing Devaluation Expectations	55
	Devaluation Expectations and Arbitrage	56
	Interspatial Effects of Devaluation on Cocoa Futures	57
	Arbitrage Opportunities during Sterling Devaluation	62
	The French Devaluation	64
Chapter 4	**Sterling Crisis Periods: Their Price Effects on Futures Markets**	**65**
	Non-Devaluation Sterling Crisis Periods	65
	The Sterling Crisis of 1957	66
	The Sterling Crisis of 1961	66
	The Sterling Crisis of 1964	73
	The Sterling Crisis of 1965	73
	The Sterling Crisis of 1966	77
	Concluding Remarks	80
	Data Appendix	83
	Notes	97
	Glossary	105
	Bibliography	109
	Index	113
	About the Author	115

List of Tables and Figures

Table

1–1	Basic Facts about New York and London Cocoa	11

Figure

2–1	Static One-Period Arbitrage Opportunities of Futures Trading between London and New York Cocoa Exchanges under Certainty	18
2–2	Intertemporal Arbitrage in Premium and Discount Markets with Inverse Carrying Charges under Conditions of Certainty: (1) $[\dot{P}^s_i < 0 < \dot{P}^f_i]$; (2) $[\dot{P}^s_i > 0 > \dot{P}^f_i]$	24
2–3	Intertemporal Arbitrage in Premium and Discount Markets with Inverse Carrying Charges under Conditions of Certainty: (1) $[\dot{P}^s_i = 0 < \dot{P}^f_i]$; (2) $[\dot{P}^s_i = 0 > \dot{P}^f_i]$	25
2–4	Intertemporal Arbitrage in Premium and Discount Markets with Inverse Carrying Charges under Conditions of Certainty: (1) $[\dot{P}^s_i > \dot{P}^f_i > 0]$; (2) $[\dot{P}^s_i < \dot{P}^f_i < 0]$	26
2–5	Intertemporal Arbitrage in Premium and Discount Markets with Inverse Carrying Charges under Conditions of Certainty: (1) $[0 < \dot{P}^s_i < \dot{P}^f_i]$; (2) $[0 > \dot{P}^s_i > \dot{P}^f_i]$	27
2–6	Intertemporal Arbitrage in Premium and Discount Markets with Inverse Carrying Charges under Conditions of Certainty: (1) $[\dot{P}^s_i < 0 = \dot{P}^f_i]$; (2) $[\dot{P}^s_i > 0 = \dot{P}^f_i]$	28
2–7	Static One-Period Arbitrage Opportunities of Futures Trading between London and New York Cocoa Exchanges under Uncertainty	33
3–1	Contract Selection Test Samples: Daily Price Movements of London Cocoa Futures	38

Figure

3–2	Contract Selection Test Samples: Daily Price Movements of New York Cocoa Futures	40
3–3	Weekly Observation Day Test Samples: Friday Weekly Price Movements of London Cocoa Futures	41
3–4	Weekly Observation Day Test Samples: Friday Weekly Price Movements of New York Cocoa Futures	42
3–5	Arbitrage Opportunities between London and New York Cocoa Futures	48
3–6	Calculation of Maximum and Minimum Levels of Arbitrage Opportunity for September London and New York Cocoa Futures during the British Sterling Devaluation Year 1967	52
3–7	Calculation of Maximum and Minimum Levels of Arbitrage Opportunity for December London and New York Cocoa Futures during the British Sterling Devaluation Year 1967	53
3–8	Comparisons in Price Movements between London and New York September Cocoa Futures during the British Sterling Devaluation Year 1967	58
3–9	Comparisons in Price Movements between London and New York December Cocoa Futures during the British Sterling Devaluation Year 1967	59
3–10	Arbitrage Opportunities of September Futures between London and New York Cocoa Exchanges during the British Sterling Devaluation Year 1967	60
3–11	Arbitrage Opportunities of December Futures between London and New York Cocoa Exchanges during the British Sterling Devaluation Year 1967	61
3–12	Arbitrage Opportunity Comparisons between September and December London and New York Cocoa Futures during the British Sterling Devaluation Year 1967	63

Figure

4–1 Arbitrage Opportunities of September Futures between London and New York Cocoa Exchanges during September Crisis Peak Period of 1957 for British Sterling   67

4–2 Arbitrage Opportunities of December Futures between London and New York Cocoa Exchanges during September Crisis Peak Period of 1957 for British Sterling   68

4–3 Arbitrage Opportunities of September Futures between London and New York Cocoa Exchanges during July Crisis Peak Period of 1961 for British Sterling   69

4–4 Arbitrage Opportunities of December Futures between London and New York Cocoa Exchanges during July Crisis Peak Period of 1961 for British Sterling   70

4–5 Arbitrage Opportunities of December Futures between London and New York Cocoa Exchanges during November–December Crisis Peak Period of 1964 for British Sterling   74

4–6 Arbitrage Opportunities of September Futures between London and New York Cocoa Exchanges during July–August Crisis Peak Period of 1965 for British Sterling   75

4–7 Arbitrage Opportunities of December Futures between London and New York Cocoa Exchanges during July–August Crisis Peak Period of 1965 for British Sterling   76

4–8 Arbitrage Opportunities of September Futures between London and New York Cocoa Exchanges during July–August–September Crisis Peak Period of 1966 for British Sterling   78

4–9 Arbitrage Opportunities of December Futures between London and New York Cocoa Exchanges during July–August–September Crisis Peak Period of 1966 for British Sterling   79

Foreword

"Bad money drives out good." Gresham's law is one of the oldest in economics science, long predating Sir Thomas Gresham. If you offer the world three nickels for a dime, the odds are certain that you are going to get a lot of dimes and soon run out of nickels. Nature abhors a vacuum; but the good lady's aversion to nothingness is itself as nothing in comparison with her impatience at a sure-thing arbitrage situation.

The present study illustrates and confirms these basic principles. So long as the British pound is tied to gold by a firm buy-and-sell offer of the British government, and the American dollar is similarly tied to gold, the exchange rate between the dollar and the pound cannot deviate from simple parity except within the narrow range of the so-called gold-export and -import points set by the small cost of transporting gold from one country to the other. From the end of Napoleon's war to the beginning of the Kaiser's war, pickings were mighty slim for arbitragers. When the Bretton Woods system was set up for post–World War II international finance, the mistake was made of setting narrow limits within which exchange rates could fluctuate around their parity ratios. But it is one thing to formulate a system in the hills of New Hampshire and another to have it work that way in the following quarter century. Repeatedly the pegged exchange rates broke down in crisis. In economics, coming events cast their shadows before them. When in 1948 I foresee that the pound is going to be devalued relative to the dollar, I can make a bundle by selling the pound short in favor of the dollar. In effect, I put up a little, borrow much, taking considerable risk on myself if my leveraged position is mistaken, and after so many days make a colossal profit. But suppose there are a lot of people like me: selling the pound short for future delivery will depress its price for future contracts; hence, the intercompetition of similar speculators will reduce the juiciness of the kill for each.

As Dr. Dominguez realized when he set out to write an MIT doctoral dissertation on how anticipations of coming exchange rate depreciation will affect the prices in London and New York of the same commodity—say, cocoa for present spot delivery or for future delivery next December or the following June—the purchasing power parity doctrine must apply with special force to standardize commodities that are easily transportable between countries. The doctrine of purchasing power parity, made popular by Gustav Cassel at the time of World War I but already implicit in Ricardo, was designed to help economists predict, on the basis of comprehensive index numbers of all prices, where a floating exchange rate was likely to settle down once the authorities decided to return to a viable steady parity. But Keynes and others soon reduced the doctrine to little more than a statement about arbitrage in connection with single commodities that move easily in trade.

What then did Dr. Dominguez set out to measure? And how did the results turn out in comparison with expectations? He knew that *after* the pound gets permanently depreciated relative to the dollar, the London prices of cocoa must have risen permanently relative to the New York prices of cocoa by approximately the amount of the exchange rate change. (Approximately, because there are costs to shipping cocoa across the Atlantic.) He reasoned that in those periods when informed people were apprehensive about a depreciation in the immediate future, the prices of cocoa futures contracts for months ahead should reflect this anxiety. From economic theory he was able to predict the direction that an expected devaluation should have on the spreads between London and New York prices for the same future delivery dates. Collecting data and running them through the computer, he had the chance to test theory against fact.

The reader of this book will see that the theories of economics passed the test of experience with flying colors in this case. Not every Ph.D. candidate is so lucky!

A study like this is not designed as a manual to tell you how to get rich. (I met a shrewd commodity investor recently who told me that he had made some good profits by following just these considerations in the 1971 period when President Nixon suspended convertibility of the dollar into gold. But he did not have to read a book to figure out how it was to be done.) A study like this is worth while for its scientific interest. First, and least important in this area, such a study confirms that there is such a thing as economic law—a view not always conceded by the vulgar masses. But, most significant, the economist studies the forces of arbitrage in order to understand the equilibrium price relationships that must prevail if people are *not* to be able to reap profits in a one-way sure-thing fashion. Moreover, an arbitrager in these Dominguez markets is not engaged in any absolutely sure thing: he cannot at the same instant take his money to one window of a bank with his left hand and withdraw from another window with his right hand, ending up after a complete and instantaneous cycle with more money than he started out with. There are two kinds of errors: not foreseeing a devaluation that is coming, and foreseeing a devaluation that is never going to come. Therefore, the daily fluctuations in the price spreads across space give us a peek, not into the future itself, but so to speak into the minds of the informed participants of the market place.

Economic research points beyond itself. Now that we are moving beyond Bretton Woods and into an era of greater exchange rate flexibilities, there will be many more dissertations to write, relating commodity-price spreads to forward-interest spreads and to the prices of currency futures on the new exchanges that are bound to come into existence.

Paul A. Samuelson

Cambridge, Mass.
March, 1972

Preface

Devaluation has historically been the subject of recurrent attention and concern. One central issue in recent years has been the realignment of par values exchange rates of the leadingn industrial countries. For the first time since 1933 the United States has been placed in a position where the drain on its gold reserves and the increase in foreign-held short-term dollar claims have required U.S. government officials to initiate a revaluation of gold.

On December 18, 1971, a meeting was held at the Smithsonian Institute to negotiate the realignment of official exchange rates. The task was complicated by the need for a differential rather than uniform adjustment, an adjustment between balance-of-payments surplus countries and balance-of-payments deficit countries. The United States' dollar, exchanged for 105 or more currencies of the world, was out of balance with only three or four; if it were devalued to be brought into balance with these three or four currencies, it would be put out of balance with its one hundred other trading partners.

On December 20th the devaluation of the U.S. dollar became official, the United States agreeing to raise the price of gold from $35 per ounce to $38 per ounce—an 8.57 percent increase and an overall currency adjustment of 12 percent. This was to take us away from trade protectionism, reduce unemployment and permit removal of the ten percent surcharge on imports.

Historically devaluation has occurred when a country may be experiencing persistent balance of payments deficits, prolonged unemployment, or both. Government officials visualize devaluation as a panacea for these difficulties. They reason that the devaluing country's goods and assets become cheaper and the rest of the world's dearer, leading to an increase in exports and capital inflows and a decrease in imports and capital outflows, and resulting in a reduction of the deficit and unemployment.

This stimuli may be short lived, however, because other nations may follow suit very soon after. Because a country has the power to establish an exchange rate, *ipso facto* it has the power to alter and by the stroke of the pen multiply its gold reserves. It is this arbitrariness of devaluation that causes speculative momentum to mount when a currency is displaying prolonged weakness. Speculators and arbitrageurs buy and sell forward and futures contracts expecting to profit from an official exchange revision.

The purpose of this study was to determine the impact devaluation has on futures markets. Most studies of devaluation have traditionally focused on the relative price changes which occur between the devaluing country's imports and exports and those of the rest of the world, without distinguishing devaluation's economic effects on markets where commodities and commodity contracts can be bought and sold for future delivery.

In Chapter 1 the evolution and institutional characteristics of organized commodity exchanges are discussed, with emphasis on the institutional developments of futures markets, and the legal and economic aspects of futures trading.

Participants in futures markets are generally manufacturers, processors and growers of farm products whose intentions are either to capitalize on or protect themselves against price movements by taking active positions. Futures markets are distinct from other types of commodity markets—only a small percentage of all the contracts traded in an organized futures exchange are consummated by delivery, due to the fact that unlike other goods transactions, the vast majority of commodity traders purchase futures contracts with no intention of receiving delivery of the actual commodity.

Chapter 2 focuses on arbitrage, developing general sets of arbitrage models with respect to time and space. Arbitrage strategy is discussed in terms of an intertemporal and interspatial decision associated with the equilibrium price spread; arbitrage activity is investigated within the context of the conditional assumptions of time and space and of the degree of foreseeable certainty. The effects inverse and positive carrying charges may have on the spot futures relation are examined within a discount and premium market situation.

Four general types of arbitrage are introduced: (I) Static One Period Arbitrage Under Certainty; (II) Dynamic Two Period Arbitrage Under Certainty; (III) Static One Period Arbitrage Under Uncertainty; and (IV) Dynamic Two Period Arbitrage Under Uncertainty. From these models a general arbitrage incentive model is developed which serves to measure empirically through time the interspatial price relationships between the New York and London Cocoa Exchanges during the Sterling Devaluation of 1967 and during Sterling crisis periods in which devaluation was not realized.

Chapter 3, which discusses the price and the interspatial spread momentum caused by the 1967 British Sterling devaluation, inquires whether devaluation transmits its price effects spatially between closely related markets for the same commodity. It also examines the types of arbitrage activity ignited by expectations of devaluation and a general change in the interspatial equilibrium basis range. In dealing with devaluation's spatial effects on interconnected markets, the technique used to measure actual spread deviations and the opportunity for arbitrage is in some sense similar to the empirical methods used in determining interest arbitrage.

Chapter 4 seeks to compare interspatial spread behavior during devaluation and non-devaluation periods. An examination of price spread trends during non-devaluation periods might indicate whether arbitrageurs expect a forthcoming change in the equilibrium basis range during periods of Sterling crisis. The Sterling crisis periods which are examined are the 1957 September crisis, the 1961 July crisis, the 1964 November-December crisis, the 1965 July-August crisis and the 1966 July-September crisis.

Grateful acknowledgment is extended to Paul Samuelson for the opportunity to study under his genius and for his helpful supervision of my doctoral dissertation, a manuscript which has contributed importantly to this book.

Robert Solow and Lester Thurow were very helpful in their comments and willingness to serve on my thesis committee. I have also profited from an earlier association with Paul Cootner who patiently introduced me to the mystical world of futures markets. I would also like to thank the Study Center of Business Economics and Finance of the U.C.L.A. Graduate School of Management for providing financial assistance for this study.

I am deeply grateful to Richard Eckaus for his counsel and sincere interest on my behalf during my tenure as a graduate student at M.I.T. I would also like to acknowledge *mi amigo simpatico,* J. Fred Weston, for his socratic patience and encouragement. To my father, John R. Dominguez, Sr., I give thanks for teaching me the worth of industry.

Finally, I wish to express deep indebtedness to my wife for her tremendous contribution to the writing of this book. She has paused thoughtfully over each word, expression, and idea that it contains, and has made a great many helpful suggestions. She has also participated most fully in the arduous task of designing and drafting the manuscript's illustrations. To Perry and Tammy, my thanks for accepting me as an absentee father. In addition, appreciation must be expressed to Miss Patricia Anderson for her talents as a research assistant and to Mrs. Theresa Davis for her accurate typing of the manuscript and her unending willingness to accept it on short notice.

1
The Evolution and Characteristics of Futures Markets

Historical Development of Futures Trading

Modern futures exchanges developed by a process of gradual evolution. "The first use of futures trading was recorded in Japan around 1690."[1] Shoguns, members of a Japanese feudal class, were accustomed to maintaining high standards of living and often issued receipts against rice that was being grown in the fields. In turn, merchants anticipating future needs in grain would buy the receipts against their expected needs. Eventually these tickets developed as a form of currency.[2]

Occidental history, on the other hand, discloses no definite time and place for the first transaction of deferred delivery of goods.[3] However, there is reason to believe that the establishment of market fairs in the Champagne district of France during the early twelfth century did introduce the time dimension into commercial transactions.[4] Medieval Europe came to rely on the gathering of merchants who could be expected to arrive with their cargo of goods at designated times and places and remain for several weeks or several months to do business with the local populace or with one another. From the Champagne fairs in mid-France developed specified commodity agreements between given parties, which probably, as some economic historians believe, were word-of-mouth contracts that could not be transferred to others, but which were nevertheless negotiable contracts of specified quantity, quality, and time of delivery. Later, as further refinements in trade practices evolved, the feature of transferability was introduced through a negotiable instrument, which became known as a "fair letter." Traveling merchants would arrive at the trade fairs with little more than samples, to avoid the risk of carrying large inventories of gold, silver, or other equally valuable merchandise. Their transactions were based on future delivery commitments for the specified commodity. Through the use of the fair letter, delivery of the prescribed merchandise could be drawn against an authorized inventory source. The fair letters were related to a specific trade and were tenderable in much the same manner as a draft on a bank. From an accountant's operational point of view, the fair letter could be viewed as a precursor of the negotiable instrument currently known as a bill of exchange.[5]

By the early 1800s, a premature form of futures trading in commodities such as food grains, oilseeds, and coffee had developed in several market centers, notably Liverpool, Chicago, Antwerp, Amsterdam, and Osaka.[6] However, trading in contracts for commodities specifying deferred delivery did not become formalized until around the middle of the nineteenth century. With the introduction of the time dimension into contractual arrangements, the practice of selling on a "to arrive" basis evolved in the grain and cotton trades of both the United States and the United Kingdom. It was from commodity traders' desire to have "regular quoted prices" for forward contracts and for uniform trading practices that the organization of early commodity exchanges came into existence. By 1859, trading in contracts for future delivery was well developed, and in 1870 and 1880, New York and London had established their first organized commodity future exchanges.[7]

Exchanges came at a time when the trading of commodities against cash transactions ceased to be a sufficient means for meeting the needs of a rapidly growing economy. Negotiable instruments had to evolve to bridge the gaps in distance and time involved in the flow of commodities from the producer to the consumer. The consequence of this need was the evolution of commodity futures markets, in which commodities are traded on the basis of uniform specifications rather than on sample, and may be purchased or sold well in advance of actual possession.[8]

Modern Futures Trading

Today modern commodity trading is conducted on either a "cash" or futures delivery basis. Within the vernacular of the market, the term *cash markets* is treated synonymously with the term *spot markets*, which denotes that immediate fulfillment of a contract is intended.

Contrary to the popularly held belief, the chief legal distinction between spot and futures markets is not the element of time involved in the delivery of a commodity. Although transactions in spot markets are most often for immediate delivery, they may also be transacted for "forward" or "to arrive" delivery, in which case a definite delivery date is specified on the contract. In general, a spot contract will state a time range for the month of delivery. To quote one trading source, "Actually a huge volume of business today is conducted on this [forward or to arrive delivery] basis."[9]

In the same manner, futures contracts may be specified for delivery during a fixed time interval within a current month. But contract arrangements of this type can be terminated within a short period. Thus, from a legal point of view, "the chief difference between cash and futures markets lies in the form of the contract used as opposed to the delivery periods involved."[10]

In spot commodity markets, commodities are bought and sold in terms of specific grades and lots determined by the interaction of buyers and sellers. In futures markets, commodities are transacted on the basis of standard contracts established by organized commodity exchanges. These contracts cannot be altered for or through individual transactions, nor can they be modified so far as prices and delivery months are concerned.

In today's modern exchanges, trading is initiated at trading rings, or as they are sometimes called in grain exchanges, trading pits. Generally, there are individual trading rings for each commodity traded. Surrounding these trading rings are blackboards registering all commodity transactions, with price quotations printed by a ticker that resembles the stock ticker. The trading floor is linked to various brokerage firms by direct wires. These direct wire systems connect most of the large metropolitan commodity trading centers.

In the early futures exchanges, the principal commodities that were traded for deferred delivery were grains and cotton. Today, a large number of new commodity contracts have been added to futures trading. These include cocoa, sugar, rubber, wool tops, coffee, fishmeal, flaxseed, cottonseed, millfeeds, lead, zinc, copper, tin, soybeans, orange juice concentrate, pork bellies, and so forth. Some of these commodities are short-lived in futures trading, or in the parlance of the market, they "die on the vine," because of the lack of trading interest. This was particularly true with fishmeal futures, which were discontinued on the London commodity exchange during the latter part of 1967. Other commodity futures are inactive temporarily but at a later time come to life again. An example of this would be pork bellies futures.

Studies are often conducted in the various futures markets to determine the feasibility of establishing futures trade in additional commodities, and accordingly, new commodity futures are introduced. This was evidenced in 1969, when apples and plywood made their debut. Not all commodities, however, are well suited to futures trading. Tobacco, fuel oil, and gasoline, for example, all failed to adapt to the demands of futures trading. The question that therefore arises is, "What makes certain commodities suitable for futures trading and others not?" One source answers in this manner:

To provide a suitable trading medium for a futures market, a commodity must meet certain qualifications. It must be sold in bulk; it must be interchangeable, susceptible to grading, and relatively imperishable. In addition, demand and supply must be uncertain, so that it is subject to wide price fluctuations from time to time, and the futures market must enjoy substantial trade acceptance.[11]

Futures Trading Participants

Individuals who trade in futures typically fall into two categories:

1. Hedgers, who take a position in futures markets as a means of insuring themselves against price risk.
2. Speculators, who hope to profit from the expected variation in futures prices.

Among speculators there are the floor traders, otherwise referred to as scalpers, who try to profit from the daily change in prices by initiating and closing a trade position within the same day. Although scalping is not legally restricted to exchange members, nonmembers are prevented from "in-and-out" trading transactions because of the higher commission and clearing cost they must pay.

Other types of speculators in futures trading are the "straddler," or "spreader," and the arbitrageur.[12] They are individuals who hope to capitalize on temporary price disparities. Spreaders try to profit from deviations in the price spread between different futures in the same commodity for a given market, or between different commodity markets. Arbitrageurs are traders who simultaneously buy and sell futures of the same commodity and delivery month in two different markets. Their transactions can take place either in the same country or in different countries. The wool market, as an example, was discussed at a futures trading seminar by Robert L. Raclin, of Paine, Webber, Jackson and Curtis. He pointed out that among the wool markets of Australia, London, and New York there may be discrepancies in price based on the tariff differentials; when supply and demand are such that the domestic price is exceeded, market fluctuations allow arbitrage. A wool center in Yorkshire has an arbitrage exchange, which takes advantage of the three futures markets.[13]

Occasionally trade straddles are made between two rival commodities such as wheat and corn, or cottonseed oil and lard. Straddle and spread trading are especially profitable for the trader who is in the upper income tax brackets, because he thereby obtains certain tax advantages. In spread trading, situations may develop that

1. Offer the possibility of both deferring the tax and converting short-term capital gains into long-term capital gains.
2. Reinstate tax losses for which the five-year period that they can be deducted from ordinary income is expiring.[14]

Determination of Futures Prices

Prices for commodity futures are determined by "open outcry," as in a public auction. On most of the commodity exchanges, the trading session is started by a special "call." The call procedure serves to establish opening prices for all delivery months in a systematic manner. Each trading month is called out in succession, and offers to sell or buy are made for that trading month only. Sometimes sales transactions are not realized at the time of the initial call. However, after the call is completed, regular trading does commence. The call procedure is generally repeated at least two or three times during each trading session.

The hours of the trading session will vary among commodities and exchanges both nationally and internationally. Futures trading is not permitted before or after an official trading period, and unexecuted orders remaining after the closing gong have to wait for the beginning of the following day.[15]

Sharp price changes, which characterize futures markets from day to day, week to week, and month to month, depend on an array of supply and demand factors. For instance, changes in expected harvest prospects occasioned by unexpected drought, frost, or other adverse weather conditions make it continually difficult to predict available future supplies. Also, disturbances created by man, such as wars, mining strikes, and the threat of nationalization, cause futures prices to gyrate. And in grain markets, governmental price support activities have a strong influence on price behavior.

Demand prospects are also subject to random shocks such as changes in rival or complementary commodity prices, shifts in taste, and fluctuations in business cycles. Each random variable directly or indirectly influences a commodity's consumption. Other demand disturbances come from portfolio adjustments such as the speculative commodity buying that often develops from expectation of a currency devaluation or its realization.

This sensitivity of futures prices to random shocks necessitates regulation of price variations on United States commodity exhanges by the bylaws of the organized exchanges.[16] One price control is the "maximum daily limit," which restricts daily price changes during a trading session. Similarly, most commodity exchanges institute a daily price variation limit, which is calculated either upward or downward from the previous day's closing price. At times the maximum price range may be double the daily price variation limit. Another control on price movements in futures markets is the regulation concerning minimum fluctuations restriction. Under exchange bylaws, futures are permitted to fluctuate in price by a set fractional amount. For example, New York accra cocoa futures are allowed to vary in price by one hundredth of a cent per pound, which is the equivalent of $3.00 on a single 30,000-pound contract.

In futures trading, price spreads between different delivery months are often considered indicative of a commodity's market conditions. For instance, distant delivery months may be quoted at either a premium or a discount over nearby months. The trading of a futures contract at a premium would be interpreted as indicating a possible supply shortage during that delivery month. Also under normal conditions, the permium differential would indicate the carrying charges for the commodity and would include storage, insurance, and credit cost. Price deviations beyond the carrying cost differential seldom persist, since speculators are constantly watching for profitable arbitrage or straddling opportunities.

Trading Volume

All commodity exchanges publish daily volume figures that are intended to give the breadth of the market for a particular commodity.[17] If the volume in trading is small, the hedging function of the futures market diminishes, "as the placing or lifting of even moderate hedges may be possible only at considerable price concessions."[18]

The total volume of trading in commodity futures has been steadily growing over time. In 1939, in the United States alone, futures trading amounted to 2,423,623 contracts. In 1962, the volume of futures trading on all U.S. commodity exchanges had increased to 5,179,975 contracts, according to the Association of Commodity Exchange Firms, Inc., of New York.[19]

In contrast with the behavior of the U.S. stock market in the 1969 recessionary downturn of the economy, the futures market was experiencing a boom year. As one brokerage house declared, "Big Board volume is down 2% from a year ago and the Amer 11%. With [futures showing] a record 7,960,000 contracts traded in the first nine months, the nation's commodity exchanges are 20% ahead of last year's pace."[20]

Contractual Arrangements

The futures commodity contract is a legal agreement to deliver or accept a definite quantity and quality of a particular commodity during a specific month at an established price. It is a legal commitment and comes under the jurisdiction of the exchange concerned. The seller has the legal right to deliver, on due notice, the physical commodity at any time during the delivery month stated on the contract. In turn, the buyer is under obligation to accept physical delivery against full payment according to the rules and procedures of the commodity exchanges. However, the buyer does have the option to terminate his futures contract holding, through the "offsetting transaction" of selling a futures contract in the same delivery month specified on the contract; this procedure is commonly known as switching.[21]

Although only a small proportion of futures transactions are consummated in delivery, this does not change the commitment of the contract. As a consequence, one cannot rightfully describe a futures contract as an *option*, a term that is commonly but incorrectly used to describe a futures contract. Since futures transactions do not usually result in the exchange of actual commodities, futures trading can probably best be thought of as dealing in the rights to a commodity; these rights may or may not be exercised. The only optional element of a futures contract is the stipulation that the seller may decide, given the specified delivery month of the contract, what day of the month to make delivery on and what grade of commodity to deliver.[22] This is often referred to in trader's jargon as the seller's option.

During the early stages of institutionalizing futures trading, a test case challenged it as a form of gambling. The decision handed down by the United States Supreme Court was that

trading in commodity futures does not constitute gambling. (Justice Holmes of the United States Supreme Court in an appeal of the case of Christie Grain & Stock Co. et al. v. Chicago Board of Trade, 1905, 798 U.S. 236).[23]

The Court's decision was as follows: Given that commodity exchanges provide adequate facilities for sellers or buyers to make or receive delivery, the assumption is made that actual delivery was intended or contemplated, and if realization did not take place, it was due to the exercise of choice.

The principal features of a modern futures contract are as follows:

1. It is a legal transaction for a stipulated quantity of a given commodity.

2. It stipulates a specific grade of commodity.
3. It gives the seller the choice of making delivery on any date between the specified limits established by an exchange.
4. It ensures enforcement of the contract through cash margins that are deposited by each of the contracting parties.

Deferred Delivery Grades

The grade of the commodity to be delivered, commonly referred to as the basis, or contract grade, is determined by the price. The contract grade is typically the grade in widest commercial use. The notion of a grade basis stems from the fact that commodities traded on exchanges have various grades that are tenderable, but at price differentials. If the commodity delivered is not of the contract grade, but tenderable under exchange specifications, then the delivery must be made by the seller at a price that is at a discount or is a premium of the contract price.

The tenderable grades of a futures contract will vary on different organized exchanges, and so will the methods of determining the price differences. One of the interesting phenomena in futures markets has been that if tenderable grades are too numerous and are in concurrent circulation, those of inferior value tend to drive those of higher value out of circulation, and the inferior grades tend to be delivered against futures contracts. Tenderable grades are not restricted to a small proportion of the total supply of a commodity because of the vulnerability a commodity may have to price manipulation.

Commodity grading is done generally in accordance with the regulations and bylaws of an organized exchange. For example, the No. 10 sugar futures contract grade specifications established by the New York Coffee and Sugar Exchange states that delivery should be made in raw centrifugal cane sugar based on 96-degree average polarization, which is the contract grade. However, depending on whether it is the New York exchange or the London exchange, additional quality standards may be imposed, such as moisture, ash, grain size, filterability, color, geographical origin, and governmental decree. In the United States, only sugar permitted to be processed or consumed under a quota or an allotment plan decreed by the U.S. government can be delivered against the No. 10 contract, a stipulation that explicitly excludes Cuban sugar.

Grade Price Differentials

The organized sugar exchanges in New York and London have the responsibility for establishing the price premiums and discounts for polarization and quality deviations from the basis. Although the method of determining price differential may vary from one exchange to another, there are two principal types of pricing differentials. They are the fixed differential and the variable differential.

A characteristic example of the fixed price differential is the hides futures formerly traded on the New York Commodity Exchange. The contract grade was a light natural cowhide with four other grades deliverable at the basis price. These four other grades carried premiums ranging from $1\frac{1}{4}$ cents to $\frac{1}{2}$ cent per pound. Variable differentials are also used in the trading of cotton futures. "The grade differentials for deliveries on cotton futures contracts are determined on the basis of average commercial differentials prevailing from day to day in bona fide spot markets, officially designated by the secretary of agriculture under the United States Cotton Futures Act."[24]

Delivery Months

A futures contract in most commodities specifices delivery in accordance with a given month and a specific unit of trading.[25] The trading range between months varies from twelve to eighteen calendar months. This means that a position in futures contracts can be taken on commodity deliveries as far in advance as one and a half years. Each futures contract designates one specific delivery month in a given year. For instance, New York and London December cocoa listed for 1969 could not have been traded against a December contract scheduled for 1970 delivery. Futures trading in most commodities centers on four to six actively traded delivery months, while other contract months experience little activity. In silver futures, the most actively traded contract months are January, March, May, July, September, and December, whereas October and November are comparatively quiet trading months.

One protection a seller has against unexpected delays in transportation is his right to make delivery during any time within the designated delivery month. The physical delivery of a commodity transacted through a futures contract is affected by transfer of "warehouse receipts." In certain instances, some commodity exchanges permit delivery on freight cars within the switching limits of specified cities. Delivery points are mostly permanent sites designated by the various commodity exchanges. The number of delivery points may, however, range from one to a substantial number depending on the type of commodity contract.

Margin Requirements

Margins on commodity trades are cash deposits required of either clearinghouse members or commodity traders. Margin requirements for futures trading are distinctly different from those for securities. Equity trading on organized stock exchanges can be transacted on a cash or margin basis, while in contrast, commodity trading on organized futures exchanges is rarely transacted on an outright cash basis.[26] The function of margins in stock transactions is to meet the legal requirements for buying stocks or bonds on credit, known as buying on margin. Commodity margin buying differs in the amount needed as a margin deposit and in the non-interest payment cost of the commitment. A buyer does not pay an explicit interest cost on the difference between his margin deposit and the full value of the quantity of the commodity specified by the futures contract. This stems from the fact that a contract is transacted for future delivery, and full payment is not due unless and until delivery is made.

In commodity transactions, there are two principal types of commodity margins:

1. Margins that brokerage firms require from their clients.
2. Margins that clearinghouses require from their members.

Typically, clients' margin requirements are higher than the margins of clearinghouse members. Even so, the margin that brokerage firms require from their clients is relatively small as compared with stock security margins: 10 to 20 percent of the purchase value as opposed to 50 to 90 percent.

Another difference between futures and stock margins is that futures margins may vary, whereas stock margins remain relatively constant over short periods of time. Moreover, if commodity exchanges allow the operation of trade accounts, as they differ from speculative accounts, bylaws regulate "maximum limits" of credit extension rather than deposits of margin.[27] Because brokerage firms must deposit and maintain cash margins with the clearinghouse, the brokerage firm attempts to protect itself by securing original margin deposits from its clients. These must be supplemented by "additional," or "maintenance," margin if the market price moves adversely.[28]

Original margin deposits will vary in accordance with the specific commodity, its prevailing price, market conditions, and the type of commodity account. A call for additional margin is generally issued when the original margin has been reduced to 75% of the initial margin by a change in the market price. On frequent occasions, the Clearing House Association will raise margin requirements as a way of stabilizing erratic price behavior. At present, on cotton exchanges, margin supports are directly tied to variations in the market price of futures, whereas in the grain exchanges, margin changes are still initiated only if it is believed that conditions warrant it.

Cocoa: New York and London Exchanges

The cocoa bean is cultivated in tropical regions, with the largest producer the African country of Ghana, and Nigeria and Brazil running second and third in importance. Cocoa production typically shows a distinct seasonal pattern, in which three-quarters of the year's harvest takes place during the months from October to February (main crop), and the remainder is harvested in May through July (mid-crop). The Ghana harvest of cocoa (accra) is purchased from cocoa farmers at a fixed price by the Cocoa Marketing Board and is sold and exported fairly rapidly to the principal northern consuming areas of the United States and the United Kingdom. Rapid handling is necessitated by the cocoa bean's tendency to spoil if stored for long periods in the tropical regions. Because of the deterioration factor, some buyers have optioned to transact forward sales, a contract that covers cash commodities to be shipped and delivered at some specified future date. Early purchasing figures of the Ghana Cocoa Marketing Board, which are indicative of the harvest size, form the principal basis for initial estimates of the entire accra crop. Also, statistical sampling and reports cerning crop disease and weather conditions serve for accra forecasting purposes. Crop forecasts are issued by two principal sources, the Food and Agricultural Organization of the United Nations and an international cocoa dealer, Gill & Duffus Ltd. The United States is the largest consumer and importer of cocoa. It utilizes two hundred forty thousand to two hundred eighty-five long tons annually. The United Kingdom is the second largest consumer, utilizing almost half of the United States quantity.

"Cocoa price movements can usefully be separated into three categories: long-term, intermediate-term, and short-term. Each of the three classes of price fluctuations can be identified with its own causal mechanism."[29] Cocoa prices in the short run, aside from being influenced by long-run and intermediate forces, are also affected by "technical factors relating to speculative activity in London and New York cocoa futures markets . . . short-term month-to-month price fluctuations in part reflect alternating tides of bullish and bearish speculative enthusiasm in the world's cocoa markets."[30] Generally, speculative interest in the cocoa market tends to focus its attention for prolonged periods on one or two background developments that may have significant influence on future cocoa prices.

The futures contract unit for accra cocoa is 30,000 pounds net of cocoa beans in original shipping bags. The basis quality is Standard Grade and Growth. The standard grades of accra tenderable in both exchanges are

Accra Types: Ghana
               Bahia
               San Thomas, fine or superior
               Ivory Coast, fermented, main crop
               Coast Rican, fermented
               Panama, fermented

All other tenderable grades are deliverable only at differential fixed by the exchanges, which may vary anywhere from $\frac{1}{4}$ cent or $\frac{3}{14}$ pence per pound premium to one cent or $\frac{6}{7}$ pence discount. Quotations on the New York Cocoa Exchange are in cents and hundredths of a cent per pound. The minimum fluctuation in price is referred to as a point, in which one point change in the value of a cocoa futures contract amounts to $3.00; and the fluctuation of one cent, or 100 points, amounts to $300.00 per contract.

On the London Cocoa Exchange, the minimum price fluctuation is recorded in terms of six pence (6d.) and the contract value of a point fluctuation amounts to £2.10.0 per contract. One notable difference between the New York and London cocoa exchanges is that trades on the New York exchange during any one day are not permitted to be made at prices varying more than one cent per pound above or below the previous closing price, whereas on the London exchange there exists no maximum daily trading limit.[31] Contracts are traded in for delivery in the current month and fourteen subsequent calendar months. The hours of trading are 10:00 A.M. to 3:00 P.M. daily, Monday through Friday.

The information that follows in Table 1–1 describes the specific exchange requirements for London and New York cocoa futures trading.

Table 1–1
Basic Facts about New York and London Cocoa[a]

	New York Cocoa	*London Cocoa*
Location	New York Cocoa Exchange	London Cocoa Terminal Market Association
Trading hours	10:00 A.M. to 3:00 P.M. (N.Y. time)	5:00 A.M. to 8:00 A.M. and 9:15 A.M. to 12:00 noon (N.Y. time)
Contract size	30,000 pounds (13.4 long tons)	5 long tons (11,200 pounds)
How prices are quoted	Cents and fractions of a cent per pound (e.g., 27.05¢ per pound)	£ per ton
Minimum price variation	1/100¢ per pound = $3.00	1/2 £ = $6.00
Value 1¢ or 1 shilling price movement	1¢ per pound = $300.00	1 £ = $12.00
Trading limits for daily price movements	1¢ ($300.00) above or below previous close	20 shillings per cwt. ($240.00 per contract) above or below previous close. This is followed by a 30-minute recess. Thereafter, trading resumes with no limits.
Regular margin on trades		
Original	$1200.00	$500.00
Maintenance	$ 900.00	$400.00
Straddles and spreads		
Original	$ 700.00	$250.00
Maintenance	$ 500.00	$250.00

[a]Source: Woodstock Inc. Market Newsletter (June 23, 1969), p. 4.

2

The Temporal and Spatial Elements of Arbitrage

With the extension of traffic in space and with the expansion over ever longer intervals of time of prevision for satisfying material needs, each individual would learn, from his own economic interests, to take good heed that he bartered his less saleable goods for those special commodities which displayed, besides the attraction of being highly saleable in the particular locality, a wide range of saleableness both in time and place. (Karl Menger, 1892)[1,2]

Definition and Description of Arbitrage Activity

Arbitrage, a derivation of the French verb *arbiter*, which means "to decide" or "to determine," is used to describe the determination or measurement of price differences that exist for the same commodities, securities, or currencies at a given point in time or in one or more locations. The person who determines or measures the difference in price is referred to by the French term *arbitrageur* or its anglicized equivalent *arbitrager*, or *arbitragist*.[3]

Prices for commodity futures may differ because of differences in contract maturity or in market location. There are therefore two types of arbitrage—intertemporal and interspatial. Intertemporal arbitrage, which results from differences between current cash or spot prices and the current price of futures contracts, is traditionally visualized as the simultaneous purchase and sale of commodities. This type of transaction is commonly referred to in the literature as hedging, if the purchase and sale involves a spot and futures contract, or spreading, if it involves between-month futures. Interspatial arbitrage, in which transactions take place between two or more different markets, is characterized by the simultaneous purchase and sale of equivalent commodities in the different markets.

The economic function of arbitrage is to balance demand and supply conditions through time and space. The disparity in prices over time and space indicates to the arbitrageur temporal and spatial supply and demand conditions. On the basis of this information, the arbitrageur buys of the surplus of one commodity exchange or contract maturity in order to supply the demand in another exchange or maturity. By buying and selling commodities through time and space in this manner, the arbitrageur serves as an agent in the equalization of commodity prices and in the distribution of commodities both interspatially and intertemporally.

Arbitrage as described in the commodity trade literature is the simultaneous purchase and sale of the same quantity of the same commodity in two different markets, either in the same country or in different countries. Arbitrage in futures is therefore initiated to take advantage of what is believed to be a temporary intertemporal or interspatial disparity in prices.

Sometimes in the trade literature, the terms *arbitrage*, *straddle*, and *spread* are used interchangeably. However, purists do choose to differentiate the meanings of the three terms. *Spread*, in the pure sense, is the simultaneous purchase and sale of a contract for a given commodity in one delivery month against a contract of equal size in another delivery month. *Straddle* is intended to describe the transaction in which an individual is long in one commodity and simultaneously short in a different commodity; for instance, the straddler buys a March wheat contract and sells short a March corn contract. Arbitrage in its purest form customarily describes a simultaneous long transaction in one market and a short position in another, for example, a long transaction in the New York Cocoa Exchange and a short position in the London Cocoa Terminal Market Association, or vice versa.

Intercontinental arbitrage has become quite active in recent years, as illustrated in the case of wool. In wool futures trading, there is a constant surveillance of the London, Sydney, and New York markets. Arbitrage positions are initiated when arbitrageurs believe that one of the above market's relative price is too low or high in comparison with one or both of the other futures markets.[4] Keeping within the old adage, they try to buy in the cheapest market and sell in the dearest, or they buy dear when they expect the price to get dearer or sell cheap when they expect the price to get cheaper. They expect that in the end the spread in prices will move towards a profit vantage.

Currently, there are active cocoa futures markets in New York, London, and Amsterdam. The volume of trading in Amsterdam, however, is much smaller than the volume of business in New York and London. The New York Cocoa Exchange conducts the largest volume of trading and maintains the greatest "open interest," that is, the number of contracts that remain outstanding.

Arbitrage and Devaluation

These cocoa futures markets will not always move in a parallel price fashion to one another. Local disturbances or increased trading interest in one of the markets will often alter price relationships. One example of local disturbances' having a greater impact on one market than on other commodity exchanges is that in which a country's currency is expected to undergo exchange revision. One trade study on sugar showed that in 1967 the threat of devaluation of the pound sterling and its realization encouraged arbitrage between New York and London, with sugar futures figuring in currency speculation.[5] Another study on wool tops futures foresaw a similar situation in that field with changes in currency values. The fear of devaluation of the pound sterling was expected to cause traders in wool tops to increase buying before the inflationary effects of devaluation would set in.[6] They could well be summed up in the words of a Merrill Lynch cocoa study: "The reasons why the arbitrageur should hedge against the risk of a revision in the pound/dollars exchange rate."[7]

Historically, devaluation of the pound has resulted in an upward shift in commodity prices, and cocoa buyers have had the incentive to buy before cocoa values would appreciate to new levels. Devaluation expectations have influenced the behavior of both those who did and those who did not plan on accepting physical delivery. Domestic speculators and holders of physical inventories who expected prices to increase due to devaluation have been expected to be bullish in their market behavior. Their long position in futures can be explained by the following:

1. Expectation of a rise in prices and the wish to capitalize on the price appreciation.
2. A wish to minimize the risk of a decrease in the purchasing power of their liquid asset holdings from an exchange depreciation.

In addition to characterizing the activities of the arbitrageurs, this type of market strategy probably describes best the trade interest of cocoa processors, handlers, growers, shippers, manufacturers, wholesalers, and retailers, in their use of hedging as a means for minimizing price risks in inventory management, or for gaining a margin of certainty towards better profits. More specifically, the shipper makes forward commitments for cocoa to be shipped from incoming crops, and buys futures to protect himself against market changes pending the completion of his transactions in actual cocoa. The importer and the merchant make forward sales of a specific kind of cocoa for specific shipment or delivery, and also buy futures as a protection against market changes pending the purchase of the actual cocoa in the producing country. The manufacturer, on the other hand, buys futures to protect himself against sales of manufactured products for which, at time of sale, he does not own the necessary actual cocoa. The secondary user of manufactured products buys futures as market protection, pending the placing of orders for the actual products(cocoa, butter, liquor, and so on) that he expects to buy. Any great surge to buy futures in London, say, is inclined to reduce activity in New York and Amsterdam.

The Arbitrage Decision

Because futures trading between joint but spatially separated markets involves the dimensions of time and space, the formulation of an arbitrage strategy at any given point in time must incorporate both an intertemporal decision and an interspatial decision. The intertemporal decision requires that an individual can (a) determine the equilibrium price spread between the spot price and futures price in both markets 1 and 2; (b) determine if the spot future relationship represents either positive carrying charges (contango) or inverse carrying charges (normal backwardation) in both markets 1 and 2; and (c) determine the proper intertemporal arbitrage strategy, given the establishment of (a) and (b).

The interspatial decision requires that an individual must (a) determine what the equilibrium price spread between markets 1 and 2 is; (a) determine whether the actual spread is equal to the equilibrium spread or at a premium or discount therefrom; and finally, (c) determine the proper interspatial arbitrage strategy given the establishment of (a) and (b).

General Types of Arbitrage Transactions

Considerations of (1) time and space and (2) the degree of foreseeable certainty are of primary importance in the arbitrage transaction. One conventional notion regarding arbitrage transactions that overlooks the time factor is summarized by the adage "Buy cheap and sell dear." This notion simplifies arbitrage by ignoring the time required for joint market adjustments of prices, spreads, and arbitrage incentives, and for the arbitrage decisions to be carried out.

Even though a minimal time factor is involved, the simple type of arbitrage described above can be thought of as static, or one-period, arbitrage. In one-period arbitrage, each transaction between arbitrageurs and non-arbitrageurs is conceived of as happening at a moment in time, and all adjustments are assumed to be instantaneous. The transaction should be thought of as timeless, since its initial and terminal periods take place concurrently. Therefore, interspatial equilibrium values and the temporary deviations from these values are significant in static arbitrage, while the times required for the reestablishment of equilibrium and for the arbitrage transaction itself are not significant.

Another type of arbitrage would be that in which time is treated as an interval rather than a single moment. This type of arbitrage transaction can be thought of as two-period arbitrage. In two-period arbitrage, account is taken of the time period involved in price or spread movements from an initial period to a terminal period. These periods may be thought of as discrete values in time representing trading periods in which t say, is the initial trading period and $t + k$, $k = 1, 2, \ldots, n$, is the terminal trading period that closes the two-period arbitrage transaction. The initial period would be the initiating of an arbitrage position—the simultaneous buying and selling of a cocoa futures in New York and London respectively. The second or terminal period would be the opposite—the simultaneous transaction of selling in New York and buying in London to offset the balance of the first period transaction before the delivery dates.

To introduce the element of time into an arbitrage transaction, we take into account the time period involved in a price movement towards a new level, or the actual spread's movement towards its equilibrium level. Adding the dimension of time also raises the question of time lags in adjustments of actual or anticipated spread changes. For instance, if the price differential between London and New York widens, taking the actual spread outside and above the equilibrium spread, there may be time lags between exchanges. These time lags cause one exchange to respond more quickly than another in its price adjustments, to correct deviations between the actual and the equilibrium spatial price spreads.

Also, the treatment of time in the arbitrage transaction allows us to plot the course of a variable, such as arbitrage incentive, through time. In this sense, two-period arbitrage can be thought of as dynamic arbitrage. In two-period arbitrage, the exogenous and endogenous variables are defined at specific time points. For instance, the price of London December futures cocoa is distinguished at time t from its price at time $t + k$. That two-period arbitrage includes time as an integral part allows us to trace the path of a variable such as arbitrage incentive from one point in time to another, and during periods in which devaluation expectations may prevail and are not realized.

The second aspect of an arbitrage transaction has to do with the degree *that future changes are correctly foreseen* by arbitrageurs. One convenient assumption is that arbitrageurs have perfect foresight of interspatial and intertemporal price movements: that they know with complete certainty equilibrium spread values between time and space, they can accurately foresee price movements between markets, and they can respond to correct any deviations from these equilibrium values. On the other hand, in practice arbitrageurs do not have perfect foresight. They do not know interspatial and intertemporal price and spread movements with exact certainty, but they have some notion of a range of expected values. Therefore their knowledge of the length of an arbitrage transaction of the movement of the spot futures in London/New York price differentials is only tentative. Arbitrage judgments as to when to enter the two markets, how long to maintain an arbitrage transaction, or how much a futures price will move in relation to its related spot price or its spatial counterpart in London or New York will be based on information the arbitrageur considers probable rather than certain.

When these aspects of time and the degree of foresight accuracy are combined, arbitrage transactions fall into four types, according to the accompanying chart. Most commodity arbitrage transactions will be one of the four types depending on the assumptions made about time and the degree of certainty for which future changes are correctly foreseen.

Types of Arbitrage Transactions	Absolute Foreseeable Certainty	Probable Foreseeable Certainty
Static, or one-period, arbitrage	I	III
Dynamic, or two-period, arbitrage	II	IV

Sometimes an arbitrage transaction may comprise a mixture of the four types. To treat the distinctions among the four types of arbitrage, it is necessary to discuss each case separately.

Case I: Static Arbitrage under Conditions of Certainty

Case I, static, or one-period arbitrage under conditions of certainty, is the case usually presented in most introductory textbooks on economics. To cite Paul Samuelson in his second edition:

In a well-organized competitive market, there tends to be at any one time and place a single prevailing price. This is because of the action of professional speculators or arbitrageurs who keep their ear to the market, and as soon as they learn of any price differences, buy at the cheaper price and sell at the dearer price, thereby making a profit for themselves—at the same time tending to equalize the price.[8]

In one-period arbitrage under certainty, we assume that the arbitrageur initiates and terminates an arbitrage position at one point in time. This does not mean that timing is irrelevant, but that the duration of time involved in the transaction or in price or spread movement is not an important factor in decision making. Furthermore, we assume that the arbitrageur carries out his transaction with full knowledge of the commission cost prevailing at the two different commodity exchanges, the currency conversion cost, and the "thinness" and "thickness" of both the cheaper and dearer markets at that instant in time.

In Figure 2–1, Case I is illustrated by back-to-back diagrams. This type of diagram is often used in partial equilibrium analysis of the impact of transport cost on the trade flows between two international markets. In this type of model, markets 1 and 2, which in this study are the New York Cocoa Exchange and the London Cocoa Terminal respectively, manifest their spatial separation in the relative price differences for the same grade of cocoa.[9] The spatial price relations between New York and London cocoa futures trading can be depicted by the following constraint.[10]

$$-T_{21}^{f}(t) \leqslant P_{2}^{f}(t) - P_{1}^{f}(t) \leqslant T_{12}^{f}(t) => A_{12}^{f}(t) = 0,$$

where the variables of the spatial constraint are as follows, in each case determined at time t, with f representing the maturity vector of cocoa futures, that is, $f = (1, 2, 3, \ldots, n)$:

$T_{21}^{f}(t) =$ per unit transport cost of cocoa for deferred delivery from market 2 (London) to market 1 (New York).

$T^f_{12}(t)$ = per unit transport cost of cocoa for deferred delivery from market 1 (New York) to market 2 (London).

$P^f_2(t)$ = price of market 2 (London) cocoa futures.

$P^f_1(t)$ = price of market 1 (New York) cocoa futures.

$A^f_{12}(t)$ = arbitrage incentive to simultaneously buy cocoa futures in market 1 (New York) and sell in market 2 (London).

In the above expression, the single subscript denotes the point in space, that is, 1 indicates market 1; and the double subscript indicates a flow between two points in space, that is, cocoa flows from market 1 to market 2. Whereas the double subscript serves to designate movements across space, the single superscript serves to describe ordinal delivery commitments through time. The superscript f is intended to designate cocoa futures in general, $f = (1, 2, 3, \ldots, n)$, where the sequence of numbers describes the closest delivery months to the present at time t.[11] Transport cost $T^f_{ij}(t)$, where $i = (1, 2)$ and $j = (2, 1)$, should be interpreted to include all cost of transfer freight, insurance, freight forwarder's commissions and futures trading commission cost associated with domestic and foreign, non-member and member transactions, foreign exchange conversion costs, and interest on capital tied up in transit, and so on. Arbitrage incentive is depicted by the notation $A^f_{ij}(t)$, where $i = (1, 2)$ and $j = (2, 1)$.

Arbitrage activity has similar effects on commodity flows and normal trade flows in the sense that the "spatial flow of goods is a subtraction from the net supply of market 1, and an addition to the net supply at 2, so that P_1 and P_2 will be mutually determined along with the spatial flow by the fully specified demand and supply schedules in both markets and the numerical transport costs."[12] We can also interpret the spatial trade constraint as a spatial arbitrage constraint, and by generalizing the previous expression, we can state the spatial constraint as follows.

$$-T^f_{ji}(t) \leqslant P^f_j(t) - P^f_i(t) \leqslant T^f_{ij}(t) => A^f_{ij}(t) = 0,$$

where $i = (1, 2)$ $j = (2, 1)$, and $f = (1, 2, 3, \ldots, n)$. When arbitrage incentive is positive, $A^f_{ij}(t) > 0$, the price difference between market 2 and market 1 for cocoa futures is greater than the per unit cost of transfer, $P^f_j(t) - P^f_i(t) > T^f_{ij}(t)$. The condition $A^f_{ij}(t) > 0$ will remain up until price movements reinstate the condition in which

$$P^f_j(t) = P^f_i(t) + T^f_{ij}(t) > P^f_i(t) => A^f_{ij}(t) = 0.$$

Figure 2–1 describes static arbitrage under certainty as follows. At an initial point in time when the opportunity exists for a one-period arbitrage transaction, a commodity arbitrageur, spatially trading in futures cocoa,

STATIC ONE-PERIOD ARBITRAGE OPPORTUNITIES OF FUTURES TRADING
BETWEEN LONDON AND NEW YORK COCOA EXCHANGES UNDER CERTAINTY*

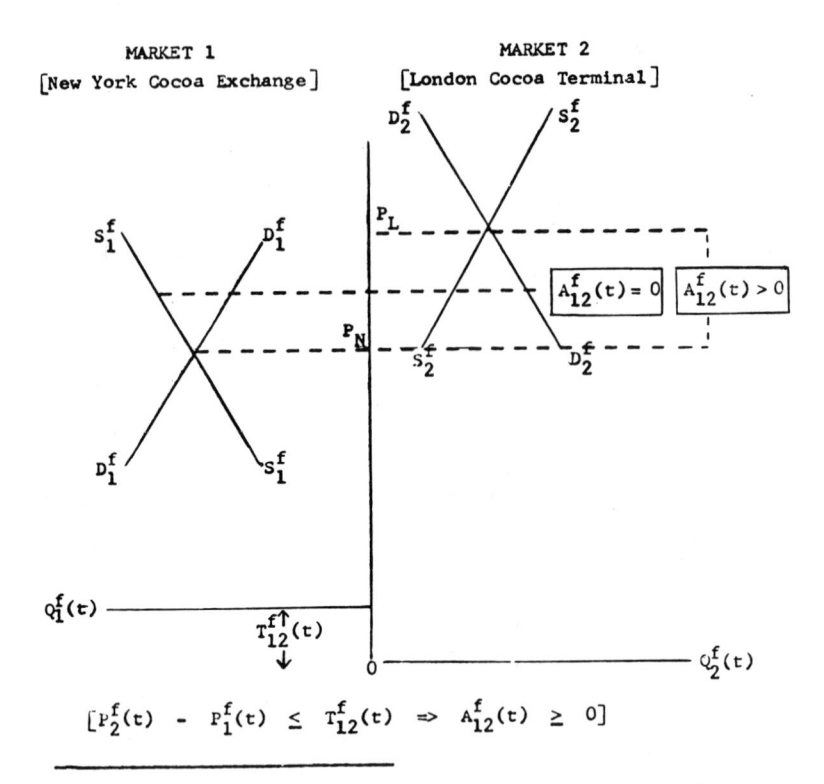

MARKET 1 [New York Cocoa Exchange]

MARKET 2 [London Cocoa Terminal]

$[P_2^f(t) - P_1^f(t) \leq T_{12}^f(t) \Rightarrow A_{12}^f(t) \geq 0]$

---

* Note: the above illustration could be extended to treat spot transactions with a forward delivery. The analysis would differ slightly only to the extent of differences in delivery periods between/associated with futures and spot transactions.

Figure 2-1.

will simultaneously buy in New York and sell in London if the price differential between markets exceeds the unit transport cost. This is demonstrated in the figure, in which the equilibrium price in London prior to arbitrage P_L does exceed the New York cocoa price P_N by more than the unit transport cost $T^f_{12}(t)$.[13] One-period arbitrage under certainty will continue to operate up to the point at which the price in London is greater than the price in New York by the margin of unit transport cost, at which time the following condition will prevail:

$$P^f_2(t) - P^f_1(t) = T^f_{12}(t) => A^f_{12}(t) = 0.$$

Case II: Dynamic Arbitrage under Conditions of Certainty

In the situation of dynamic arbitrage under certainty, Case II, the dimension of time enters into the arbitrage transaction. Here the arbitrageur strategy is planned over time with full knowledge of all conditions existing in both markets through time and space. For example, a sequence of future spread movements associated with different trading periods is clearly foreseen, and arbitrage transaction costs, joint market conditions, and price relation changes will be in accordance with a definite time-span pattern known to the arbitrageur.

In the case of two-period arbitrage, at any moment in time a well-informed arbitrageur will see the futures price at time t in markets 1 and 2 as representing an expected value of what the actual spot price will be at time $t + k$, where $k = (1, 2, 3, \ldots, n)$. From this expected value of tomorrow's spot price, the arbitrageur will determine the equality or inequality conditions that may exist between the actual and equilibrium intertemporal price spread. Between the trading periods t and $t + k$, the arbitrageur's "properly anticipated prices may fluctuate randomly."[14]

In the discussion that follows, dynamic arbitrage is analyzed intertemporally. However, the analysis could easily lend itself to the interspatial aspect as well.

At any moment in time, the following intertemporal identity will exist in a commodity market. Given $P^s_i(t) > 0$ and $P^f_i(t) > 0$,

$$P^s_i(t) - P^f_i(t) \equiv B^a_i(t),$$

which states that the difference between the spot price in Market I at time t is identical to its actual spot futures price basis.[15] To convert this identity to an equilibrium statement, we need to alter the expression to read

$$B^e_i(t) = B^a_i(t) \equiv P^s_i(t) - P^f_i(t)$$

and

$$B_i^e(t) \equiv E[P_i^s(t)] - E[P_i^f(t)] = B_i^a(t) \equiv P_i^s(t) - P_i^f(t),$$

where the variables in the above expression are defined as follows, in each case for the conditions at time t in Market I, where $I = i = (1, 2)$:

$B_i^e(t) =$ equilibrium spot futures prices basis.

$B_i^a(t) =$ actual spot futures price basis.

$P_i^s(t) =$ actual spot price of cocoa in Market I.

$P_i^f(t) =$ actual futures prices of cocoa in Market I.

$E[P_i^s(t)] =$ expected spot price of cocoa in Market I.

$E[P_i^f(t)] =$ expected futures price of cocoa in Market I.

The spot future equilibrium may also be altered to include intertemporal price conditions and therefore also "positive" or "inverse" carrying charges. Again referring to the previous variables, we may now express the equilibrium statement that explicitly treats a "carrying charge allowance" as follows:

I. Positive Carrying Charges:

$$P_i^s(t) < P_i^f(t) \Rightarrow B_i^e(t) = B_i^a(t) \equiv P_i^s(t) - P_i^f(t) < 0.$$

II. Inverse Carrying Charges:

$$P_i^s(t) > P_i^f(t) \Rightarrow B_i^e(t) = B_i^a(t) \equiv P_i^s(t) - P_i^f(t) > 0.$$

Now, it we make the assumption that the equilibrium spot futures price basis at time t is identical to the spot futures equilibrium basis at time $t + k$, where $k = (1, 2, 3, \ldots, n)$, we can show how the spot futures price relationship responds under equilibrium disturbances in a market manifesting either positive or inverse carrying charges. In this two-period time analysis, we shall still maintain the assumption of perfect foresight, and we shall also treat an arbitrage transaction that straddles a market or markets over time as taking place during a span of two periods. The initial trading period will be designated by t, and the terminal period of the arbitrage transaction will be designated by the trading period at time $t + k$.

It is important to stress that the lower-case Greek delta is identical in meaning with the capital delta, that is, $\delta \equiv \Delta$. Keeping this identity in mind, we see that the discrete incremental change in $P_i^s(t)$ with respect to t may be represented by the following:

$$\frac{\delta P^s_i(t)}{\delta t} \equiv \frac{\Delta P^s_i(t)}{\Delta t}.$$

For notational brevity, let us also identify the above expression as

$$\dot{P}^s_i \equiv \frac{\delta P^s_i(t)}{\delta t} \equiv \frac{\Delta P^s_i(t)}{\Delta t}.$$

As previously mentioned, the element of time in this case would be the duration between trading periods t and $t + k$. If at the initial trading period t, the equilibrium spot futures basis is less than the actual spread, that is, a premium market condition: $[B^a_i(t) \equiv P^s_i(t) - P^f_i(t) > B^e_i(t) > 0]$, or the basis is greater than the actual spread, that is, a discount market condition: $[B^e_i(t) > B^a_i(t) \equiv P^s_i(t) - P^f_i(t) > 0]$, then the combination of spot futures and spread adjustments we should expect under conditions of perfect certainty can be illustrated diagramatically in Figures 2–2, 2–3, 2–4, 2–5, and 2–6.[16]

These figures show intertemporal arbitrage motion between spot and futures cocoa with a maturity structure manifesting inverse carrying charges. Diagrams (a) and (b) show the spot and futures price adjustments and (c) depicts the actual spread movement necessary to eliminate a premium or discount basis deviation.

The price and spread movements associated with inverse carrying charges in a premium market are represented by the heavier or thicker line in the diagrams, and the thinner line represents similar carrying charges in a discount market. If we were to switch the labels on the vertical price axis from P^s_i to P^f_i and vice versa, and also assign negative values to the basis axis B^e_{ij}, B^a_i, [where $B^e_i(t)$ represents the negative distance from zero, equivalent in absolute discount deviational value to the positive value of $B^e_i(t)$], we could demonstrate the price and spread movement corresponding to positive carrying charges $B^e_i(t) = B^a_i(t) < 0$ in a premium and discount market. However, the discount movement of the spot and futures price, illustrated by the thinner line, would represent premium price behavior under positive carrying charges; and the premium price movement, illustrated by the thicker line, would represent discount price behavior. In the basis quadrants, the directional movement of the premium basis line would represent the basis movement under both positive and inverse carrying charges. The discount line would also correspond to the discount line associated with positive carrying charges.

The assumption of perfect foresight ensures that the representative arbitrageur can clearly distinguish the length of the arbitrage transaction. In two-period dynamic arbitrage a unique relationship, which constitutes the equilibrium basis, exists between the future and the spot price. This equilibrium

INTERTEMPORAL ARBITRAGE IN PREMIUM AND DISCOUNT MARKETS
WITH INVERSE CARRYING CHARGES UNDER CONDITIONS OF CERTAINTY

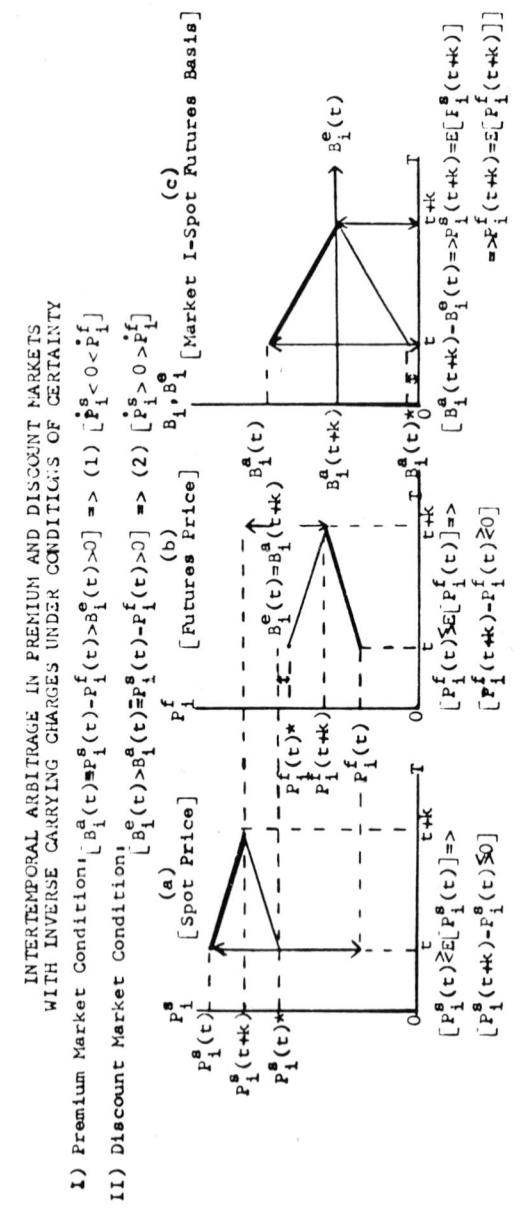

I) Premium Market Condition: $[B_i^a(t) \equiv P_i^s(t) - P_i^f(t) > B_i^e(t) > 0] \Rightarrow (1) \ [\dot{P}_i^s < 0 < \dot{P}_i^f]$

II) Discount Market Condition: $[B_i^e(t) > B_i^a(t) \equiv P_i^f(t) - P_i^s(t) > 0] \Rightarrow (2) \ [\dot{P}_i^s > 0 > \dot{P}_i^f]$

(a) [Spot Price] (b) [Futures Price] (c) [Market I-Spot Futures Basis]

Figure 2-2.

Figure 2-3.

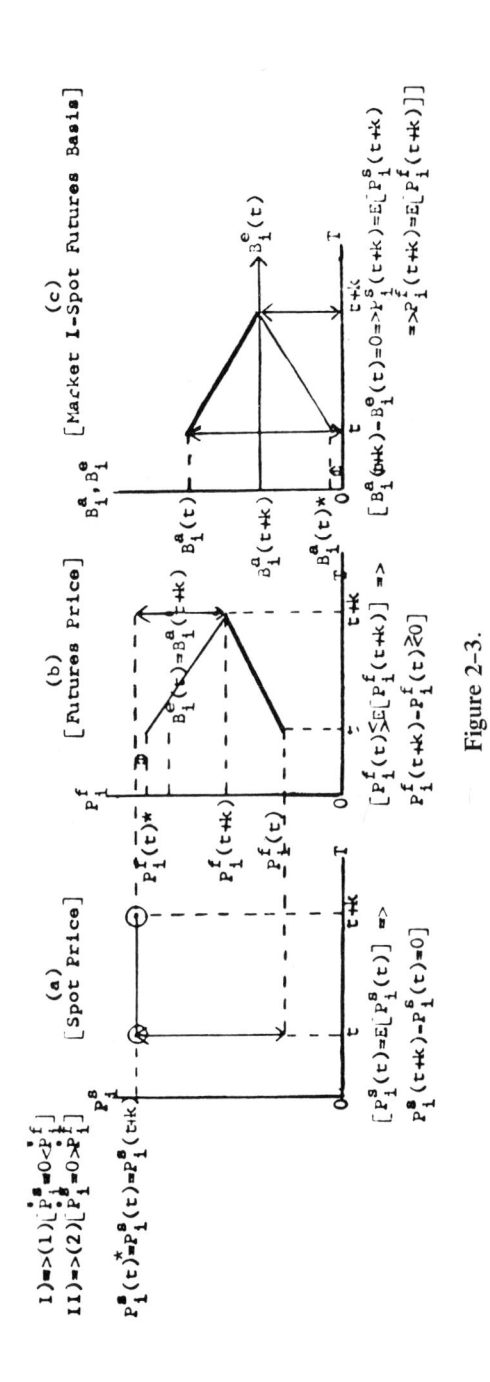

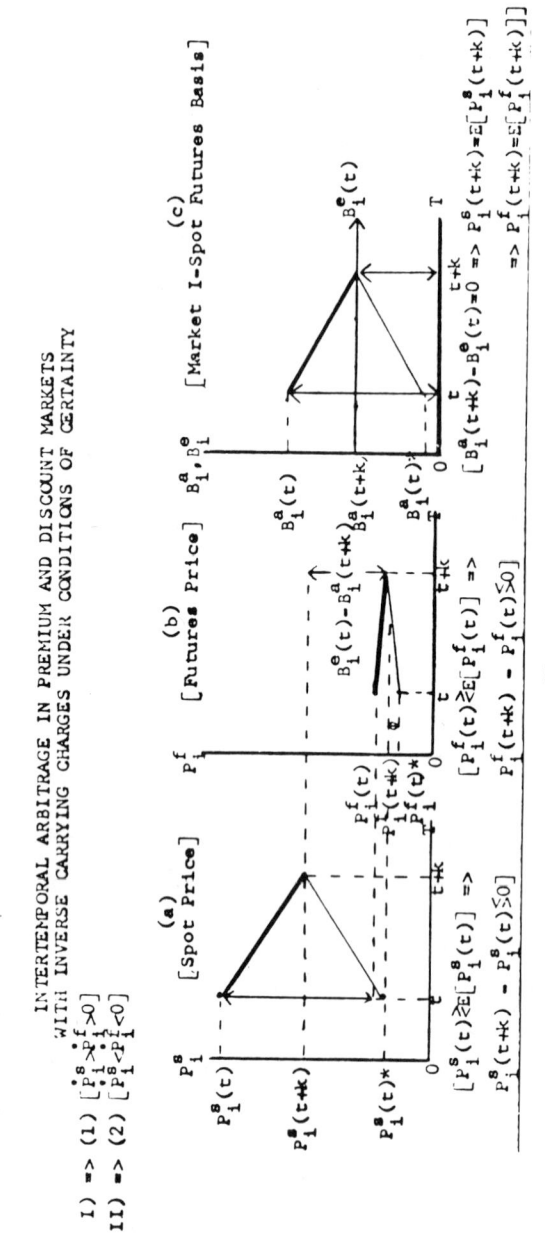

Figure 2-4. INTERTEMPORAL ARBITRAGE IN PREMIUM AND DISCOUNT MARKETS WITH INVERSE CARRYING CHARGES UNDER CONDITIONS OF CERTAINTY

I)=> (1) [$0<P_i^s<P_i^f$]
II)=> (2) [$0<P_i^s>P_i^f$]

(a) [Spot Price]

$P_i^s(t)*$
$P_i^s(t+k)$
$P_i^s(t)$

[$P_i^s(t) \leq E[P_i^s(t)]$] =>
$P_i^s(t+k) - P_i^s(t) \gtrless 0$

(b) [Futures Price]

$P_i^f(t+k)$
$P_i^f(t)$

$B_i^e(t) = B_i^a(t+k)$

[$P_i^f(t) \geq E[P_i^f(t)]$] =>
$P_i^f(t+k) - P_i^f(t) \gtrless 0$

(c) [Market I-Spot Futures Basis]

B_i^a, B_i^e

$B_i^a(t)$
$B_i^a(t+k)$
$B_i^e(t)$

[$B_i^a(t+k) - B_i^e(t) = 0 \Leftrightarrow P_i^s(t+k) \equiv E[P_i^s(t+k)]$
$\Leftrightarrow P_i^f(t+k) \equiv E[P_i^f(t+k)]$]

Figure 2-5.

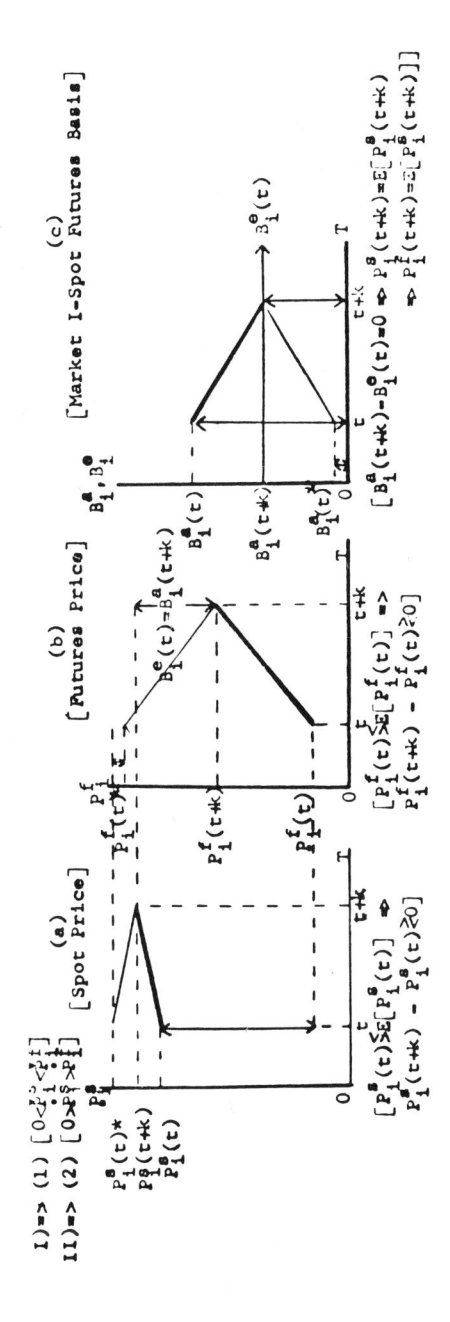

28

INTERTEMPORAL ARBITRAGE IN PREMIUM AND DISCOUNT MARKETS
WITH INVERSE CARRYING CHARGES UNDER CONDITIONS OF CERTAINTY

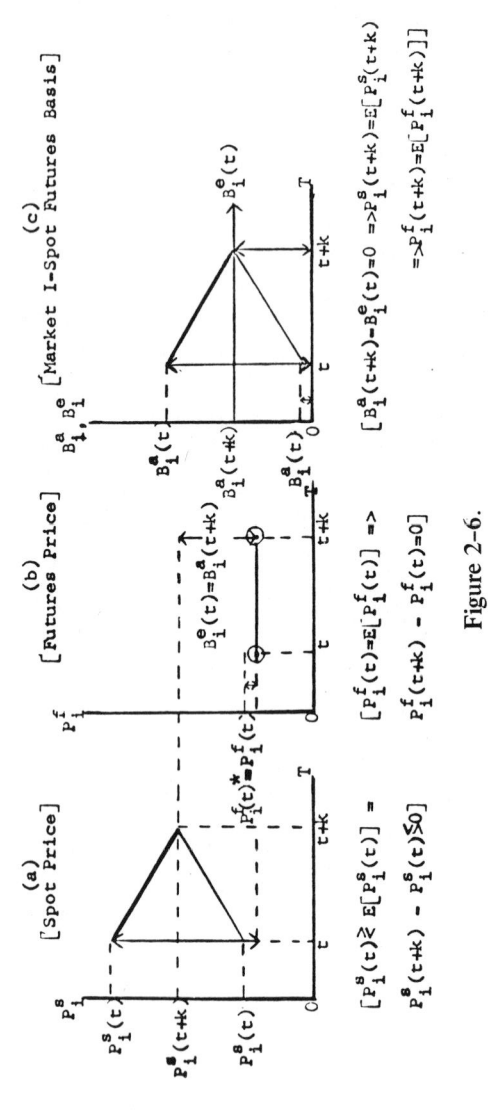

I) => (1) $[\dot{P}_i^s < 0 = \dot{P}_i^f]$
II) => (2) $[\dot{P}_i^s > 0 = \dot{P}_i^f]$

(a) [Spot Price]

$[P_i^s(t) \gtreqless E[P_i^s(t)]] =$
$P_i^s(t+k) - P_i^s(t) \gtreqless 0$

(b) [Futures Price]

$[P_i^f(t) = E[P_i^f(t)]] =>$
$P_i^f(t+k) - P_i^f(t) = 0$

(c) [Market I-Spot Futures Basis]

$[B_i^a(t+k) - B_i^e(t) = 0 => P_i^s(t+k) = E[P_i^s(t+k)]$
$=> P_i^f(t+k) = E[P_i^f(t+k)]]$

Figure 2-6.

basis is made up of expected values that are discernible to the well-informed arbitrageur at trading periods t and $t + k$ both. By discerning the proper combination of spot futures mean values, an arbitrageur can identify the correct spread deviation as premium or discount and subsequently capitalize on this temporary spread deviation.

For example, suppose a cocoa arbitrageur in two-period arbitrage correctly foresees a price discrepancy between London and New York cocoa futures in the same delivery month. He considers the price of New York cocoa futures to be significantly lower than the price of London cocoa futures. Or to state it differently, he believes that the actual London/New York price spread is too wide.

$$[P^f_2(t) - P^f_1(t)]_{\text{Actual spread}} > [P^f_2(t) - P^f_1(t)]_{\text{Equilibrium spread}}.$$

He therefore decides to simultaneously buy and sell cocoa futures scheduled for the same delivery periods in markets 1 and 2 respectively. If the spread between London and New York narrows or returns to the foreseen equilibrium spread at the terminal trading period $t + k$, the arbitrageur makes a profit through spatial arbitrage.

The interesting aspect of two-period arbitrage, whether under certainty or uncertainty, is that it combines the intertemporal with the interspatial decision in the selection of an optimum arbitrage strategy. In two-period arbitrage, a cocoa arbitrageur will vary his intertemporal decision with expected changes in the spot futures price spread. To illustrate, if the spread between spot cocoa and futures in New York is too wide, the arbitrageur will buy New York cocoa futures with the intention of selling at a later trading period when the spot futures spread has either narrowed or returned to its equilibrium spread value. In other words, the cocoa arbitrageur examines the New York price spread between cocoa spot and futures. If the actual spread is too wide or greater than the equilibrium spread at time t, the initial trading period,

$$[P^s_1(t) - P^f_1(t)]_{\text{Equilibrium spread}} \quad [P^s_1(t) - P^f_1(t)]_{\text{Actual spread}},$$

he expects that the spot futures spread will narrow as a result of

$$\frac{\delta P^f_1}{\delta t} > 0 \quad \text{and} \quad \frac{\delta P^s_1}{\delta t} \leqslant 0.$$

The second term in the equation does not include the equality sign because arbitrageurs in this example are not considered to be holding positive inventories in cocoa.[17]

If the arbitrageur has inventory holdings and conducts spot sales on a forward delivery basis (for example, an individual purchases spot cocoa at time t and he needs to await delivery at a later time but at a time shorter than the scheduled delivery of the nearest futures contract), then he can take a two-position stance in both markets. He could be short in actuals and long in futures at time t and reverse his position at time $t + k$ when the spot futures spread had narrowed as a result of either

$$\frac{\delta P_1^f}{\delta t} \geq 0 \quad \text{or} \quad \frac{\delta P_1}{\delta t} \leq 0$$

or both. However, in this case we need to make the added assumption that cocoa futures and spot prices do not move in an exact parallel manner, as is often the case in reality.

The non-inventory holding arbitrageur is principally concerned with $\delta P_1^f/\delta t > 0$ during his arbitrage transaction, for this futures price movement adds to his intertemporal profits. In contrast, if the spot futures spread adjustment is experienced solely by $\delta P_1^s/\delta t < 0$ and not by a futures price adjustment, then, abstracting for the moment from commission costs and so forth, an arbitrageur neither wins nor loses and his intertemporal profits are zero. But since Case II provides the arbitrageur with perfect foresight, this situation should not arise in two-period arbitrage under certainty. This same type of decision is important in the choice of timing and the choice of spot future spreads in the London Terminal. At the same time that the arbitrageur is buying futures at the widest margin between the price of spot and futures cocoa in New York, he is simultaneously selling London futures as a hedge, at the narrowest possible spread or at the highest futures price:

$$[P_1^s(t) - P_1^f(t)]_{\substack{\text{New York} \\ \text{actual} \\ \text{spread}}} < [P_1^s(t) - P_1^f(t)]_{\substack{\text{New York} \\ \text{equilibrium} \\ \text{spread}}}$$

Thus, if in the New York Cocoa Exchange at time t

$$[P_1^s(t) - P_1^f(t)]_{\substack{\text{New York} \\ \text{equilibrium} \\ \text{spread}}} < [P_1^s(t) - P_1^f(t)]_{\substack{\text{New York} \\ \text{actual} \\ \text{spread}}}$$

and at time $t + k$, where $k = (1, 2, 3, \ldots, n)$,

$$[P_1^s(t+k) - P_1^f(t+k)]_{\substack{\text{New York} \\ \text{equilibrium} \\ \text{spread}}} = [P_1^s(t+k) - P_1^f(t+k)]_{\substack{\text{New York} \\ \text{actual} \\ \text{spread}}}$$

an arbitrageur, under conditions of foreseeable certainty in futures price movements, will realize a positive intertemporal profit by arbitraging in New York futures. And if in the London Cocoa Terminal at time t

$$[P_2^s(t) - P_2^f(t)]_{\text{London equilibrium spread}} > [P_2^s(t) - P_2^f(t)]_{\text{London actual spread}}$$

and at time $t + k$ ($k = 1, 2, 3, \ldots, n$)

$$[P_2^s(t+k) - P_2^f(t+k)]_{\text{London equilibrium spread}} = [P_2^s(t+k) - P_2^f(t+k)]_{\text{London actual spread}},$$

again, assuming the arbitrageur foresees correctly the change in futures prices, he will receive a positive intertemporal profit by arbitraging in London futures.

In two-period arbitrage, the arbitrageur has two avenues of profit opportunity open to him, and the optimum arbitrage strategy is to capture the maximum profit in both markets. It is the summation of the two intertemporal profits that constitutes the spatial profit in an arbitrage activity where at time t

$$[P_2^f(t) - P_1^f(t)]_{\text{London/N.Y. equilibrium spread}} > [P_2^f(t) - P_1^f(t)]_{\text{London/N.Y. actual spread}}$$

and at time $t + k$, where $k = (1, 2, 3, \ldots, n)$,

$$[P_2^f(t+k) - P_1^f(t+k)]_{\text{London/N.Y. equilibrium spread}} = [P_2^f(t+k) - P_1^f(t+k)]_{\text{London/N.Y. actual spread}}.$$

Case III: Static Arbitrage under Conditions of Uncertainty

In Case III, uncertainty exists at a single point in time because the information about cost or joint market price conditions prevailing at that time is incomplete. For instance, for an arbitrageur to capitalize on a temporary deviation, he must act instantaneously. On the other hand, to ascertain all of the arbitrage opportunities that may exist among all futures and spot contracts being traded in both exchanges, he must scrutinize the information carefully and compare the profitability of each arbitrage position. Weighing the profitability of different positions takes time, and any slight lapse in time may result in a loss of the opportunity to arbitrage a one-period transaction.

The problem facing the arbitrageur, therefore, involves considering each arbitrage position as one profitable transaction in competition with other arbitrage transactions of various degrees of profitability. Frequently, the obvious arbitrage may not be the most profitable one, due to the different seasonal trading volumes associated with different contracts. Because futures prices for different delivery months will vary in accordance with positive or inverse carrying charges, the arbitrageur may find himself choosing between buying and selling strategies.[18] And because intertemporal price differentials may vary, interspatial spread deviations from a joint market equilibrium basis may also vary in accordance with the type of carrying charge gradient. Consequently, there may exist at any given moment in time an arbitrage position that dictates a simultaneous purchase in New York and sale in London, and another that suggests an opposite course.

In Case III, arbitrage behavior is similar to that of Case I except that uncertainty over foreseeable price movements causes arbitrageurs to calculate their strategy in terms of the expected values of the variables in spatial constraint:

$$-T^f_{ji}(t) = P^f_j(t) - P^f_i(t) = T^f_{ij}(t) = > A^f_{ij}(t) = 0,$$

where $i = (1, 2)$ and $j = (2, 1)$ and $f = 1, 2, 3, \ldots, n$) and $E[A^f_{ij}(t)] > 0$ as long as $E[P^f_j(t) - P^f_i(t)] > E[T^f_{ij}(t)]$; similarly, $E[A^f_{ij}(t)] = 0$ when the following condition is realized:

$$E[P^f_j(t)] = E[P^f_i(t)] + E[T^f_{ij}(t)] > E[P^f_i(t)] = > E[A_{ij}(t)] = 0$$

Case III is illustrated in Figure 2–7.

Static uncertain one-period arbitrage is also associated with the situation in which an arbitrageur responds to the prevailing quoted equilibrium price in markets 1 and 2 by attempting to simultaneously arbitrage at the previously quoted prices. But because certain "informal market barriers" exist, the arbitrageur is prevented from completing his transaction simultaneously. Possibly communication channels between exchanges, within an exchange, or between an arbitrageur and his broker are temporarily blocked, and as a result, only one side of the transaction is completed. Another side to this problem is the common difficulty of securing immediate service on the floor of both cocoa exchanges. Occasionally arbitrage may be handled by independent exchange members, who execute orders for firms that engage in arbitrage operations. These independent brokers may choose not to tie themselves up to the extent necessary to provide instantaneous service under all circumstances, unless the importance of the individual's account or the size of the transaction warrants neglect of business from other sources. In Case III, arbitrage is actually more of a nearly simultaneous transaction type, thereby introducing the first traces of price risk involved in a slightly delayed arbitrage transaction. The fact that the price of cocoa futures in one market or both may change before the arbitrageur can initiate or complete his transaction increases the risk that the price spread between the two cocoa exchanges will move against him.

STATIC ONE PERIOD ARBITRAGE OPPORTUNITIES OF FUTURES TRADING
BETWEEN LONDON AND NEW YORK COCOA EXCHANGES UNDER UNCERTAINTY*

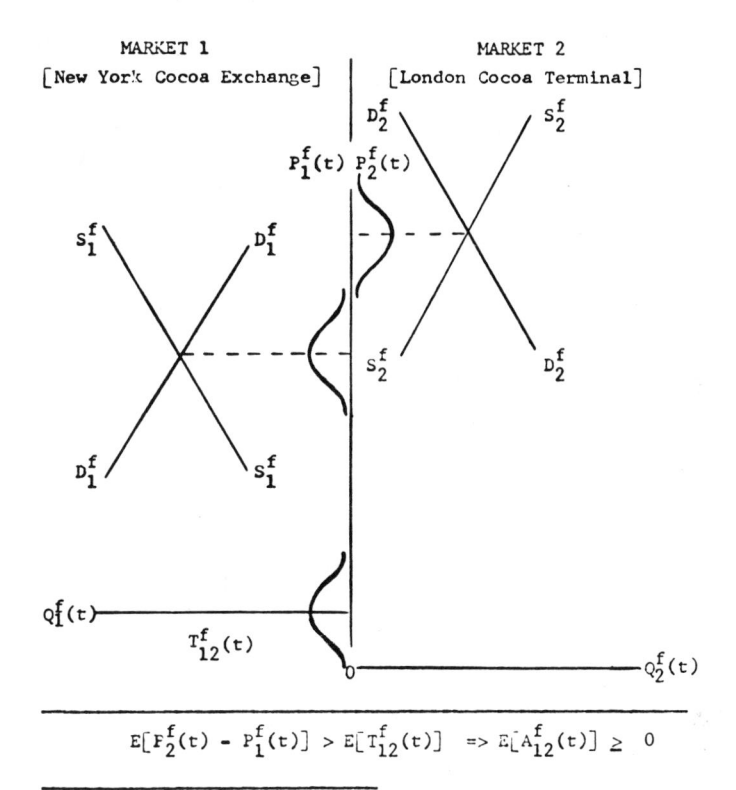

MARKET 1 [New York Cocoa Exchange]

MARKET 2 [London Cocoa Terminal]

$$E[F_2^f(t) - P_1^f(t)] > E[T_{12}^f(t)] \Rightarrow E[A_{12}^f(t)] \geq 0$$

*Note: In the above diagram the probability distribution was chosen for expository purposes rather than an attempt to assign arbitrageur expectations to a normal probability distribution. The sole intention of attaching normal curves to the vertical axis was to visually demonstrate that arbitrageurs visualize probable movements of prices and transport cost in both directions at the point in time when he attempts to arbitrage simultaneously.

Figure 2-7.

Case IV: Dynamic Arbitrage under Conditions of Uncertainty

In Case IV, the dynamic two-period arbitrage transaction under conditions of uncertainty, we have a more realistic treatment of commodity arbitrage. To the arbitrageur, the future is, in general, uncertain. Neither exact movement in futures prices nor the duration of an arbitrage transaction can be foreseen with certainty. Therefore, the formulation of an arbitrage strategy over time cannot be isolated from uncertainty except as a provisional device. This uncertainty involved in an arbitrage transaction reduces an arbitrageur's decision to an *if–then* conditional approximation instead of one of absolute certainty. Under conditions of dynamic uncertainty, an arbitrageur will initiate a two-period arbitrage position and thus straddle two markets over time if he expects the disparity between the actual spread and the equilibrium spread to be only temporary. And he sees joint market forces moving to correct this gap at an expected terminal period.

The arbitrageur's intertemporal decision to initiate a position in futures in one market when the spot futures spread is widest or in another market when the spot future is at its narrowest spread, helps to increase the probability that the London/New York spread will move in his favor and thus maximize his spatial profits.

Under conditions of uncertainty, two-period arbitrage calls for arbitrageurs to be able to distinguish what the equilibrium values in three markets are. One is the equilibrium spread associated with the New York spot futures relation, a second is the equilibrium spread between London spot and cocoa futures, and the third is the interspatial price spread between the two different cocoa exchanges, London and New York.

This type of arbitrage is essentially an arbitrage operation based on the expectation of a favorable intertemporal and interspatial price relation. But price spread movements are uncertain because prices at different exchanges or at different times may not rise and fall together; therefore time lags are thereby caused in the spread movement between and within exchanges. This, in turn, may cause an extension of the arbitrage transaction beyond its expected terminal date. Generally, the length of the arbitrage transaction will adjust to the expected value of the futures spread. If the expected London/New York spatial price differential is realized prior to the expected terminal date, the arbitrage transaction will be terminated. This means that ex-ante and ex-post arbitrage transaction lengths, as well as ex-ante and ex-post spread movements may not always be equal.

Since any sizeable change in the price differential between London and New York will affect the arbitrageur's estimate of the transaction's duration, the uncertainty associated with the time factor is compounded, even though uncertainty regarding the directional movement of the spread may decrease. Consequently, the arbitrage decision depends on the relative weight an individual assigns to these two factors—the expected length of time of an arbitrage transaction, and the expected directional movement of the spread.

Another problem that springs from the issue of uncertainty is that a pronounced transitory deviation from what arbitrageurs accept as the current equilibrium spread may be interpreted as an early signal of a change in tomorrow's equilibrium value. This is particularly true in the instance in which shipping negotiations are currently under way or devaluation expectations are present. Both of these situations could cause a widening of the London/New York equilibrium basis. Moreover, there tends to be a direct relationship between the magnitude of a transitory spread deviation and the anticipated length of an arbitrage transaction. And since any pronounced change in the price differential between London and New York will affect the arbitrageur's estimate of the transaction's duration, it adds to the uncertainty over the time factor even though it reduces the uncertainty over price or spread direction. In other words, given that no shift in the equilibrium basis is anticipated, the greater the deviation between the current actual spread and the equilibrium spread, the less the uncertainty surrounding the future expected spread movement. Yet, the greater the spread deviation, the less the certainty about the length of the arbitrage transaction. The outcome of a two-period uncertain arbitrage transaction depends on the combination of both elements, and principally on the relative weight assigned to the expected transaction's length or the expected basis movement as a determinant of the arbitrage strategy. Because of the uncertainty that encompasses dynamic uncertain arbitrage, arbitrageurs' decisions are based largely on probability.

In Case IV, the assumption of foreseeable certainty is relaxed and this requires us to substitute expected values for known values. Take the situation in which devaluation expectations are hovering around the British pound. Arbitrageurs as a group may be responding to expected spreads rather than the known spread because of uncertainty about the pound/dollar exchange revision, which would automatically cause a shift in the London/New York price differential. Arbitrage activity involving commodity futures may be responding to anticipated changes in the locational price spread between two periods, and the forecast of profits or transport costs may depend on devaluation expectations as well as on the expected future spread, the current spread, and the previous past spread. As a consequence, the structural arbitrage equations describing group behavior may have a random component because of the uncertainty that pervades the decision making of arbitrageurs.

For example, in a dynamic exact (certain) two-period arbitrage transaction, the actual spread between London and New York might exactly equal the equilibrium spread. Introduction of a random element into this spatial equilibrium condition may render the equilibrium basis equal to the actual spread plus a random term, and may achieve an interspatial equilibrium, except for the random deviation that arises from market and data imperfections. As will be seen in the empirical section of this study, the random element will serve to explain the interspatial equilibrium basis between London and New York as a range rather than a fixed unique value.

3 Devaluation: Its Effects on Futures and Arbitrage Incentive

In the cross-sectional time series investigation of devaluation's effects[1] on the joint cocoa futures markets of London and New York, the British devaluation period of 1967 was chosen as the sample observation period. Friday weekly observations were conducted for September and December cocoa futures of both the New York and London cocoa exchanges. In the empirical examination of devaluation price effects on cocoa futures, certain methodological assumptions had to be made. The discussion that follows focuses on the problems met in the attempt to measure devaluation's interspatial effects in cocoa futures prices, and on the arbitrage incentive resulting from these price effects.

The Appropriate Trading Contracts

Since the opportunity for arbitrage is a phenomenon of very short run, we have chosen to work with weekly observations. This allows us to distinguish between different discount and premium arbitrage incentive trends that might develop during a period of devaluation expectations. Weekly data enable us to associate these trends with other exogenous disturbances that are typically linked with devaluation expectations, such as crisis periods for sterling, Labor party election results, Bank of England pound support intervention, and trade balance reports.[2]

For investigational purposes, the futures contracts of September and December cocoa were selected as most representative of all futures contracts for the time period. As seen in Figure 3–1, the month of September follows closely the same price pattern of the three earlier contract months of 1967, March, May, and July, with the spread between futures showing a growing premium.[3] Typically, the spread between London futures varies from two to two and one-half shillings. In the preliminary examination of the London data, it was found that sequential delivery months separated by two-month periods behaved normally in terms of their spread premium difference. On the other hand, contracts separated by three-month periods manifested erratic spread behavior between premium and discounted differences. In the sample chosen for selecting the representative contracts, we found that by observing September 1967 cocoa, we could infer how earlier contract months would have behaved in their price movements over the observation test sample. In the case of London cocoa, one only needed to deduct approximately two shillings from the September futures price to obtain for each earlier delivery their respective price.

Although we attempted to discover if the two shillings differential between contracts and their two-month time span were related, this was never

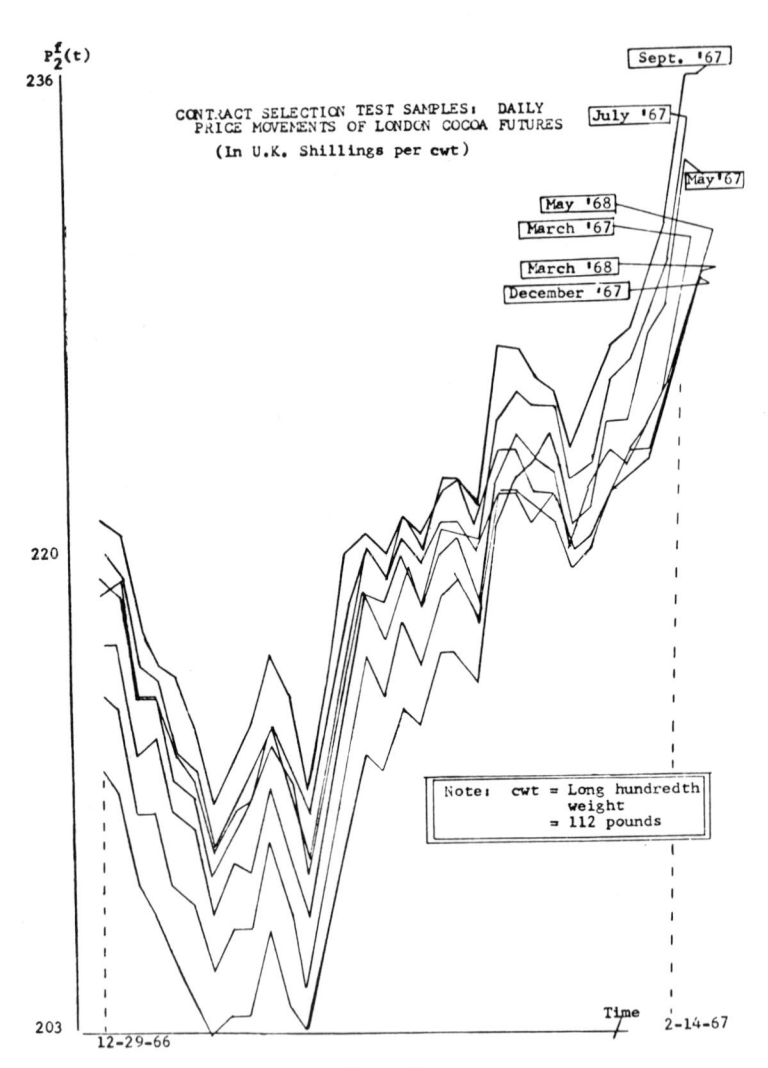

Figure 3-1.

determined. Had a correlation between monthly differentials and shilling differentials been found, it would have been possible to conclude that intertemporal transport cost in London futures is represented by one shilling. If such were the case, then the price spread beween the first four delivery months traded during any given year would generally be predictable, and from this, one could ascertain both equilibrium conditions between futures and any possible deviations from equilibrium.

As expected, there is no definite trend pattern between September and December. The spread constancy between futures does not hold true for September and December and the contract months that follow December. The spread between these contracts varies among positive, negative, and zero.

A similar sample test was conducted for New York cocoa futures; again September and December were chosen over other contract months. The cocoa futures price time series, which can be seen in Figures 3–1 through 3–4, illustrates a set of observations plotted on either a daily or a weekly basis for both London and New York. The observation sample began on Thursday, December 29, 1966 and terminated on Tuesday, February 14, 1967. This period was selected because it was considered to be free of British sterling crisis pressures and free of seasonal extremes, such as seasonal price highs and lows. Each futures contract observed during this test sample is relatively free of these seasonal factors.

In Figures 3–1 to 3–4, the points are plotted at equal intervals. The variables involved in the time series plotting are the London or New York futures price for the 1967 delivery months of March, May, July, September, December and for March and May of 1968. The plotted points indicate that:

1. Allowing for variations in premium differences, September can generally serve as a representative index of the price movement for March, May, and July trading months for 1967 delivery.
2. Allowing for "crossovers" from premium to discount, the price pattern of the futures contract for December can serve as representative of the price trend for March and May of 1968.

The contract months of September and December were selected for various other reasons. September represents the final trading month of the previous crop year, and December represents the first trading contract for the new or unharvested crop year. Also, September and December are outside of the seasonal low and high price periods of April–May and July–August respectively.

Under normal conditions, we should expect price differences between September and December to widen or narrow principally in relation to the expectations for cocoa output or consumption (grindings). If it appeared that prior to September, output would be closely matched with consumption, the September–December price differential would tend to narrow. On the other hand, if a relatively large gap existed between output and consumption going into the month of September, the September delivery

CONTRACT SELECTION TEST SAMPLES: DAILY
PRICE MOVEMENTS OF NEW YORK COCOA FUTURES
(In U.S. Cents per pound)

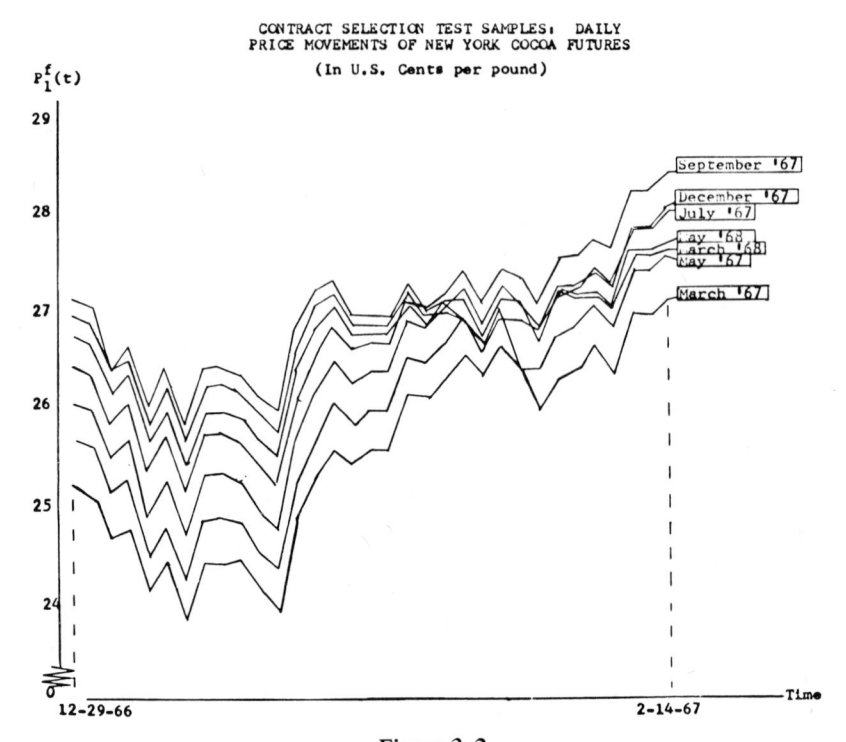

Figure 3-2.

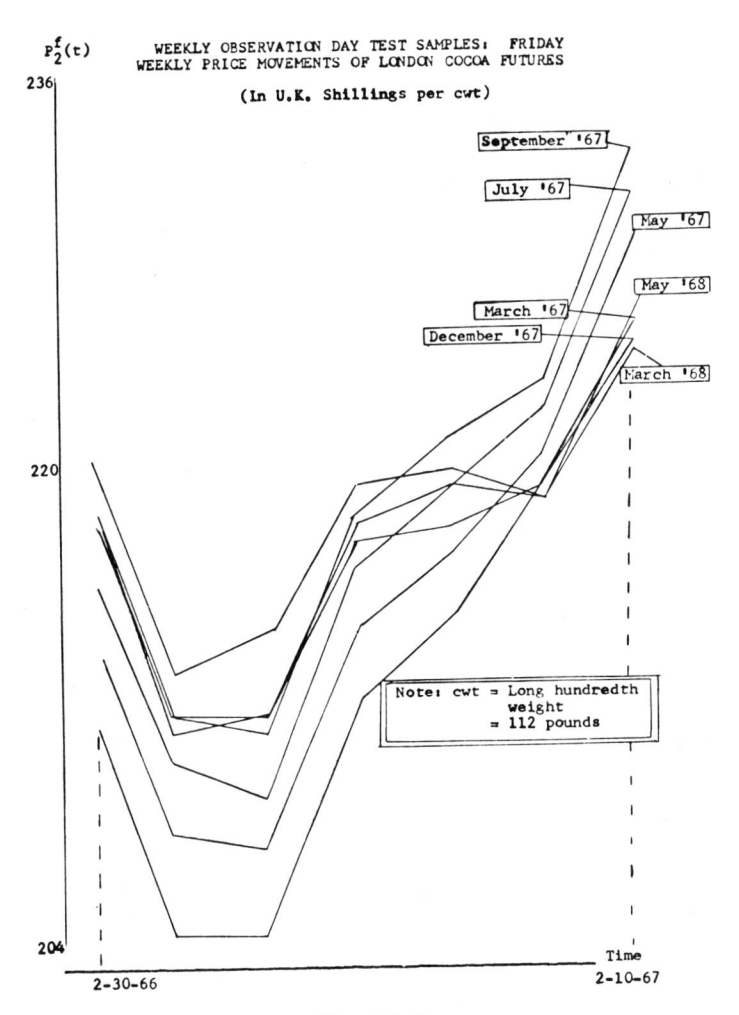

Figure 3-3.

WEEKLY OBSERVATION DAY TEST SAMPLES:
FRIDAY WEEKLY PRICE MOVEMENTS OF
NEW YORK COCOA FUTURES

(In U.S. Cents per pound)

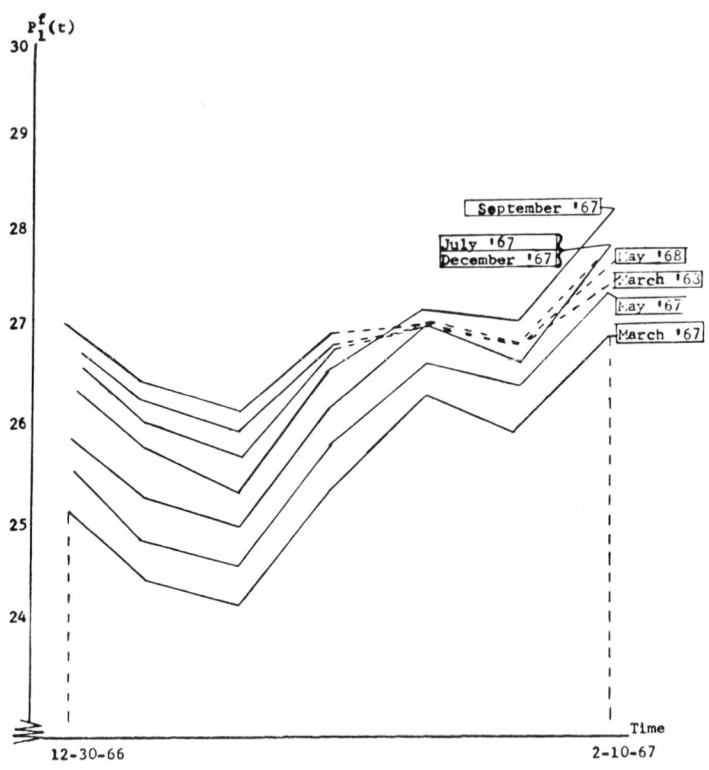

Figure 3-4.

month would tend to place September at a discount and thus tend to widen the December–September spread.

Another reason for selecting September and December futures is that sterling devaluations or crisis periods have historically culminated in the fall months. Hence, if devaluation expectations should show up, they should be seen in the futures trading of December and September contracts during the fall months. It is perhaps true that a sterling devaluation would have some effect on more distant or earlier trading months; however, it is the author's belief that September and December futures would experience the greatest price effects from devaluation of the pound. For example, sterling crisis periods have generally taken place during the Fall months. The last three devaluations that Great Britain experienced were on September 21, 1931, September 19, 1949, and November 18, 1967. Coincidentally, the periods between British devaluation have been eighteeen years apart. A naive believer in the consistency of this pattern might expect Great Britain to devalue the pound again in 1985.

Similarly, since the post-war period of the first eight sterling crisis periods, six of these crises either have begun in the fall months or have reached their greatest momentum then. Also, since the last two out of three devaluations did occur in the month of September, we might consider the September contract as a predevaluation or devaluation contract, and the December contract as postdevaluation. Therefore, as the fall approaches, we might expect to see varying price behavior such as discounts and premium changes between September and December.

Selection of the Trading Day

In choosing the weekly observation day, similar precautions against biases were exercised. Diagrams, which are not included in this study, were constructed from weekly time series graphs of Monday, Tuesday, Wednesday, and Thursday for London and New York cocoa futures from the same test sample. A comparison of each day's time series profile with the daily plotting trends of both London and New York indicated that Friday best approximates the daily futures price series for both exchanges. As can be seen by comparing Figures 3–3 and 3–4 with Figures 3–1 and 3–2, Friday does resemble reasonably well the general price trend of the two daily time series.

As in the selection of the observation contract, there were several reasons for selecting Friday as the observation day. First of all, devaluation of the pound was generally expected to occur over the weekend. This meant that devaluation expectations would most likely show up in Friday's observation. Secondly, commodity exchanges are frequently closed on Mondays, and seldom on Fridays, because of legal three-day holidays. Thirdly, in the past, when sterling devaluation has been realized over the weekend, Mondays, and sometimes Tuesdays, have been closed trading days because of the time involved in official price adjustments enacted after devaluation. If Monday had been chosen as the weekly observation day, this would have created the unnecessary problem of losing observation periods or having to switch to other days in the week in order to maintain a continuous observation test sample. At it turns out, by working with Friday weekly observations, I found the number of entry substitutions from Friday's absences was negligible. And, as previously noted, if we observe the shape of the plotted daily and weekly Friday price data in Figures 3–3 and 3–4, it is evident that Friday does resemble the general shape of the daily price trend for both New York and London. Finally, the sampling of Friday data allows us to see the week-long price adjustments after devaluation has been realized. In other words, Friday observations often represent or summarize the week's trading behavior.

Problems in the Representative Price

The attempt to observe the combination of spot and futures prices that represent the narrowest margin in one market and the widest margin in another cannot be treated properly by the available data. Therefore this study will abstain from measuring the spot futures price relation and focus its empirical attention on interspatial price behavior over time. One of the problems confronted was that there were no accessible data sources for London spot cocoa data during the year 1967. Even if the London spot data were obtainable, there would still be the problem of deciding which of three prices to observe—the high, the low, or the opening price. Ideally, if it were possible to compare the spot and futures price combinations that prevailed during the mutual trading hours of both exchanges, there would be little problem in choosing the widest and narrowest spread from among the various spot and futures price combinations. However, as this is not possible, either the opening, the low, or the high price must be chosen. Each of these three prices recorded for New York cocoa futures present certain characteristic biases. For example, if the spot prices were at a premium, it is apparent that if the spot futures spread were calculated between the premium spot and the low futures price, the widest spot futures basis would automatically be obtained. It is also true that the use of the high price would render the narrowest spot futures spread.

Another problem to consider is the lack of assurance, regardless of the price we choose—high, low, opening—that any of these prices actually prevailed during the mutual trading session of both London and New York. Furthermore, the spot price that is recorded is generally the market price prevailing at the close of the trading day.

New York Futures Price

A similar problem arises when one attempts to select the New York futures price. For example, in the attempt to approximate the correct average price that prevailed between the 10:00 A.M. opening of the New York Cocoa

Exchange and the 12:00 noon trading hour, which are equivalent to the 3:00 P.M. trading hour of the London Cocoa Terminal and its 5:00 P.M. closing hour respectively, a choice had to be made between the three alternative prices, the opening, the high, and the low. A midpoint price, constructed by adding the high and low price and dividing by two, was also considered.[4]

The reason for concern over the choice of prices to best represent these concurrent trading hours is that if arbitrage is to take place between the two exchanges, it will take place when both markets are open and arbitrage can be simultaneously transacted. By choosing to observe a price that is representative of the London and New York concurrent trading hours, the investigator makes an attempt at singling out a price that existed during two-fifths of the trading time allotted to both exchanges. If the high price of New York futures were chosen, it would automatically give a downward bias to the interspatial spread $P_2^f(t) - P_1^f(t)$. Or if the lowest trading price were used, the opposite would be true.

Another point to consider is that if either of these two New York prices were chosen, there is no way to refute the challenge that either price occurred after the London closing. However, assuming that normal trading conditions prevailed on the New York Cocoa Exchange, it is doubtful that both the high and low prices would have occurred during the last three-fifths of the trading day. This is one reason why a midpoint price was considered as a possible average price that could have prevailed during New York's first two hours of trading. There are, however, obvious shortcomings to a midpoint price in that it is difficult to determine if any arbitrage transaction per se did take place at this hypothetical price. The New York futures market may be "so thick" that any shift in price from either its low point or its high could have taken place so suddenly that no transactions were executed at a midpoint price. Also, a midpoint between the low and the high prices could have occurred outside of the arbitrage time interval of 10:00 A.M. to 12:00 noon. This is a reasonable assumption since the midpoint in time of a trading day is 1:00 P.M. rather than 12:00 noon.[5]

To avoid both upward and downward biases in the selection of an observation price and the problem of whether or not this price was an actual market price, we chose the opening price. We therefore know that it was an official quoted market price, and that it existed at a time when transactions could have been executed at both exchanges. Furthermore, there is a direct linkage between the opening price in New York and the futures price in London. One trade source has stated that the London prices indicate the figure at which New York will start trading—above or below the previous day's close—because by the time the New York market opens at 10:00 A.M., the London market will have been in session several hours, and quotations from there will have reached New York.[6]

One important matter to note is that if all three prices—the opening, the high, and the low—produce a price spread differential between London and New York that is at a premium, then we may infer that the actual price that did exist during the mutual trading hours of London and New York would also have produced a premium spread, assuming the same London price data were used. If we consider that any price movement proceeding from the opening price position in either an upward or downward direction towards its high or low must find its pathway between these two extremes, then we may conclude that the actual price that existed during the concurrent trading hours of both exchanges would have also resulted in a premium spread.[7]

However, if the use of the high price results in a discount spread, there may be no way to determine if the actual market price that prevailed between 10:00 A.M. and 12:00 noon would have produced a discount or an equilibrium spread. This is particularly true when you are working with an equilibrium band, or range, rather than a unique equilibrium value. The high price may produce an actual spread that is at a discount and the low price may, at the same time, show a premium spread between London and New York. Thus, whether the actual spread during the hours of 10:00 A.M. and 12:00 noon, New York time, was at a premium or a discount, or within the equilibrium basis range is indeterminable.

London Futures Price

For empirical convenience, the highest price was consistently picked whether it was a transacted or a nontransacted price. This was done to avoid the problem of having to work with four individual prices: the bid price, the ask price, the lowest transacted price, and the highest transacted price. The maximum and average spread between the bid and ask prices and the lowest and highest transacted prices were calculated so as to determine the upper-limit bias that might exist in the observation results of this study. As it turned out, the maximum recorded spread over a fifty-observation sample for the London September and December futures was equivalent to one shilling and sixpence (1s. 6d.), or one and a half shillings, and the average spread was sixpence. It became apparent after the data were plotted, that the use of the London highest transacted and nontransacted prices did not cause an upper bias in the arbitrage estimation to the point of disturbing the observation conclusions.

New York and London Arbitrage Incentive

One of the principal reasons for measuring the maximum and average price differences between the high and the low, and the ask and the bid, was to determine possible upper and lower limit price distortions that might exist in estimating the actual London/New York price spread. Translation of these maximum and average differences in the four prices into U.S. cents equivalence revealed that the minimum price difference between the lowest and the highest transacted and nontransacted prices was approximately equal to 0.05¢, a value that coincidentally turned out to be the average price difference as well. The maximum price difference had a value of approximately 0.14¢. Consequently, the spread estimation limits of distortion for using the highest price resulted in a range of error of 0.05¢ to 0.14¢. In terms of an inequality statement, we may say that

$$0.05¢ \leqslant \text{Actual spread} \leqslant 0.14¢.$$

These error considerations in the British data are not a casual matter. For example, let us take the equilibrium basis range $[0.75 \leqslant B^e_{ij}(t) \leqslant 1.00]$ that is used throughout the empirical work of this study. If the actual spread measured between London and New York was equal in value to 1.14¢, we could not say with certainty whether the true actual spread value had not been biased by the choice of the London highest price. It is possible that the real value could be 1.00¢ rather than 1.14¢. And if this were the case, the spread value of 1.14¢ would be interpreted as indicating that the opportunity for premium arbitrage was positive, when in reality it was zero, given the real spread value of 100.

This may be seen diagrammatically in Figure 3–5, which shows the minimum (UL', LL') and maximum (UL'', LL'') range of distortion that would result from the use of the London highest price. In Figure 3–5, LL and UL represent the upper and lower limits of equilibrium where the incentive to arbitrage is zero. The designations LL' and UL' signify the minimum error limits, and LL'' and UL'' represent the maximum error limits within the discount and premium arbitrage incentive regions. These limits are measured in accordance with the estimated error resulting from the use of the London highest transacted and nontransacted price.

The variable representing arbitrage incentive is designated as $A^f_{ij}(t)$, where $i = (1, 2)$ and $j = (2, 1)$, and reads as follows:

$A^f_{12}(t)$ = premium arbitrage incentive [buy in New York and sell in London].

$A^f_{21}(t)$ = discount arbitrage incentive [buy in London and sell in New York at time t with the expectation that the basis will be advancing upward towards the equilibrium basis range].

The interspatial equilibrium basis range that is seen in Figure 3–5 is intended to designate the upper and lower bounds for the locational price differential between London and New York where the arbitrage incentive is zero. This notion is based on a cocoa study conducted by the Cocoa Department of the Commodity of Merrill, Lynch, Pierce, Fenner and Smith, Inc., wherein they observed that when the spread between the London market and the New York market exceeds the ordinary 75 to 100 points, the situation is ripe for arbitrage. London is usually higher in price of delivery contract, reflecting differences at the time in delivery differentials

ARBITRAGE OPPORTUNITIES BETWEEN
LONDON AND NEW YORK COCOA FUTURES

$P_2^f(t) - P_1^f(t)$

Arbitrage Incentive Premium of London Cocoa
$[A_{21}^f(t) < 0 < A_{12}^f(t)]$

— — — — — — — — — — — — — — — — UL"
— — — — — — — — — — — — — — — — UL'
1.00 ─────────────────────── UL

Interspatial Equilibrium Basis Range $[A_{12}^f(t) = A_{21}^f(t) = 0]$

0.75 ─────────────────────── LL
— — — — — — — — — — — — — — — — LL'
— — — — — — — — — — — — — — — — LL"

Arbitrage Incentive Discount of London Cocoa
$[A_{21}^f(t) > 0 > A_{12}^f(t)]$

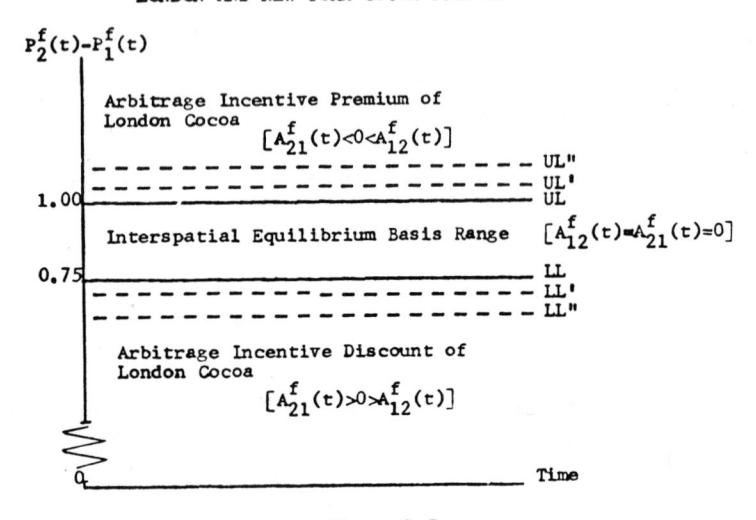

Time

Figure 3-5.

and hence in types of cocoa offered in the markets, but any unusual spread may cause selling in London and buying in New York if the London premium is high, or the converse, if the opposite situation exists.[8]

Under normal circumstances, a London/New York point spread between 75 and 100 points will not entice arbitrage activity, because such variations in spreads will not be large enough, in some instances, to offset commission charges, or the uncertainty associated with small random spread deviations that might move against the arbitrage.

The Foreign Exchange Rate and Price Conversion

In choosing among the various foreign exchange rates for price conversion purposes, the problem encountered was to choose the foreign exchange rate that gave the minimum amount of upper or lower bias to the converted price. The pound/dollar rates observed and tested were the parity, spot, 30-, 60-, and 90-day forward rates. The two rates, parity and 90-day forward rates had extreme upper bias and also lower bias. The parity rate tended to give the converted price value of London cocoa into U.S. cents a premium bias and as a result of this, it also produced an upper bias in the spread between London and New York. The opposite situation was true for the 90-day forward rate, which gave a lower spread and price bias. Except for a few negligible exceptions, the different exchange rates, beginning with the parity rate and moving towards the 90-day rate produced a definite cleavage in both spread and converted prices.[9] The 30-day forward rate was chosen because it has neither an extreme lower nor an extreme upper bias.

Further justification for selecting the 30-day forward exchange rate was that (1) it does not have the upper or lower distortions of the parity, spot and 90-day exchange rate; (2) it is a transacted rate whereas the parity rate serves more as an official nominal rate; and (3) in contrast to the spot rate, it permits financial leverage in the exchange of dollars and pounds, which is especially important to the arbitrageur who utilizes the leverage factor in futures trading.

One indication of this trading preference for forward foreign exchange in commodity arbitrage is Paul Einzig's comment that "the volume of forward exchange business arising from arbitrage in commodities is larger than generally realized. In practice, it is hardly distinguishable from forward exchange business originating through trade."[10] However, there is some doubt cast on Einzig's statement; for example:

In the United States normal spot usance is for two working days ahead but it is always possible to deal for one day value and, in United States and Canadian dollars, same day value. Settlements are normally for "compensates value" (the same value in both centers). The only exception to this is the U.S.A., where the absence of a "same day" clearing in New York means that deliveries are usually one day later, *three days later* for value Friday etc.[11]

Because of the three-day delay involved in a spot exchange transaction arising on Friday, it is conceivable that arbitrage initiated on Friday and terminated on Monday might favor spot over forward exchange. However, the issue of deposit and commission cost differences must still be considered. For instance, in U.S. dollars, the spot brokerage fee for $100,000 amounts to 6s—d, or the equivalency of $\frac{1}{400}$ of a cent in the rate. Brokerage spot deposit requirement is $\frac{1}{32}$ percent per annum from both parties involved in the spot transaction. "Customers of standing, however, are not normally required to make any down payment in respect to forward contracts. In other cases, a deposit of approximately 10 percent may be required."[12] In terms of commission differences, the margin of forward over spot may vary between $\frac{1}{8}$ cent and zero depending on the size and type of transaction. In addition, commercial houses or banks will charge an exchange commission of $\frac{1}{8}$ percent, but there is a maximum limit of six pounds approximately on the total size of the commission.

Security sterling, which was abolished on April 11, 1967, generally commanded the same price as spot sterling. Thus, if we were considering an arbitrage transaction between London and New York in security sterling, we should also examine the impact of the dollar–security sterling exchange rate by the use of the spot rate.

Therefore, taking into consideration the cost and time lag differences between spot and forward rates, it is difficult to assert positively that the 30-day forward rate would be preferred to spot in a Friday to Monday arbitrage transaction.

Possible Biases in Estimating Arbitrage Incentive

The following equation helped in finding possible upward or downward biases that might distort the estimation of the arbitrage incentive:

$$A^f_{ij}(t) = P^f_j(t) - P^f_i(t),$$

where $i = (1, 2)$ and $j = (2, 1)$. Various interspatial spreads were calculated by varying the New York futures prices (high, low, opening, midpoint) and the different pound/dollar exchange rates (parity, spot, 30-day forward, 60-day forward, and 90-day forward). By construction of different combinations of plotted time series, it was possible to separate and distinguish the maximum and minimum levels of a biased spread. The aim of this type of spread examination was to bias the spread by combining a price and exchange rate to achieve a maximum or minimum price differential. We found that by combining the spot and parity exchange rates with the New York low, the uppermost spread could be obtained.

In contrast, if you coupled the 90-day forward rate with the New York high, you would have the minimum price differential between New York and London. In Figures 3–6 and 3–7, we can see the results of combining futures prices with the various exchange rates. However, for reasons of visual clarity, only the spot rate/low price, 30-day forward/opening price, and 90-day forward/high price combinations are shown.

In Figures 3–6 and 3–7, the principal indication of the results is that only in a few cases was it questionable that the arbitrage incentive might be misinterpreted as falling within the equilibrium basis where the arbitrage incentive would be zero as a result of the use of different exchange rates. During this test sample, the majority of the $A^f_{ij}(t)$ observations fell clearly into the premium or discount arbitrage incentive region whether one chose to convert the British price by the spot, or 30- or 90-day forward rate or to use the high, low, or opening price.

The decision was made to vary New York's high, low, midpoint and opening prices while holding the pound/dollar exchange rate constant in order to see what biases might be attached to the commodity traders' price conversion formula. This formula is to determine whether the arbitrage incentive is for a premium or a discount strategy, that is, whether $A^f_{ij}(t) \lessgtr 0$. It was clearly seen that the commodity trader's formula gives an upward or spread bias.

The formula, which has been clearly described in the literature, prescribes that all one needs to do to obtain the cents per pound price equivalency between London and New York is to divide the London price by 8 if the rate of exchange is $2.80 per pound or by 9.33 if the rate of exchange is $2.40 per pound.[13,14]

Impact of Devaluation Expectations on the Basis

To understand the behavior of the price spread between London and New York during the British devaluation of 1967, it was necessary to visualize the spread's periodic motion as an equilibrium process moving towards a new expected equilibrium level.[15] Under these circumstances, the expected future equilibrium basis will differ with changes in the arbitrageur's devaluation expectations. This stems from the fact that if there is an official revision in the pound/dollar exchange rate, the relative value of cocoa between London and New York will automatically change.

Definition of an arbitrage activity during a period of devaluation expectations calls for making certain assumptions about arbitrage activity within the context of an expected change and a constant equilibrium basis. The first assumption is that actual spread deviations from the equilibrium basis develop from random disturbances that can be associated with local and international supply and demand conditions. The second assumption is that changes in the spread between New York and London are independent of devaluation expectations. Under this second assumption, temporary spread deviations from the equilibrium basis range are assumed to be directly related to devaluation expectations. If the first assumption prevails in both

52

CALCULATION OF MAXIMUM AND MINIMUM LEVELS OF
ARBITRAGE OPPORTUNITY FOR SEPTEMBER LONDON
AND NEW YORK COCOA FUTURES DURING THE BRITISH
STERLING DEVALUATION YEAR OF 1967*

[Spot, 30 and 90 Day Forward Currency Conversion Rates]

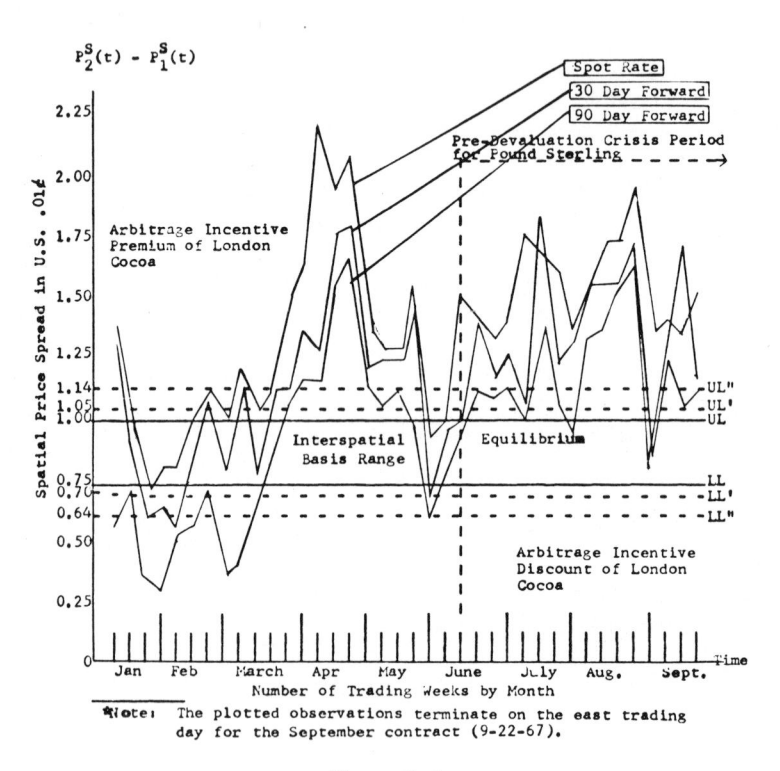

Figure 3-6.

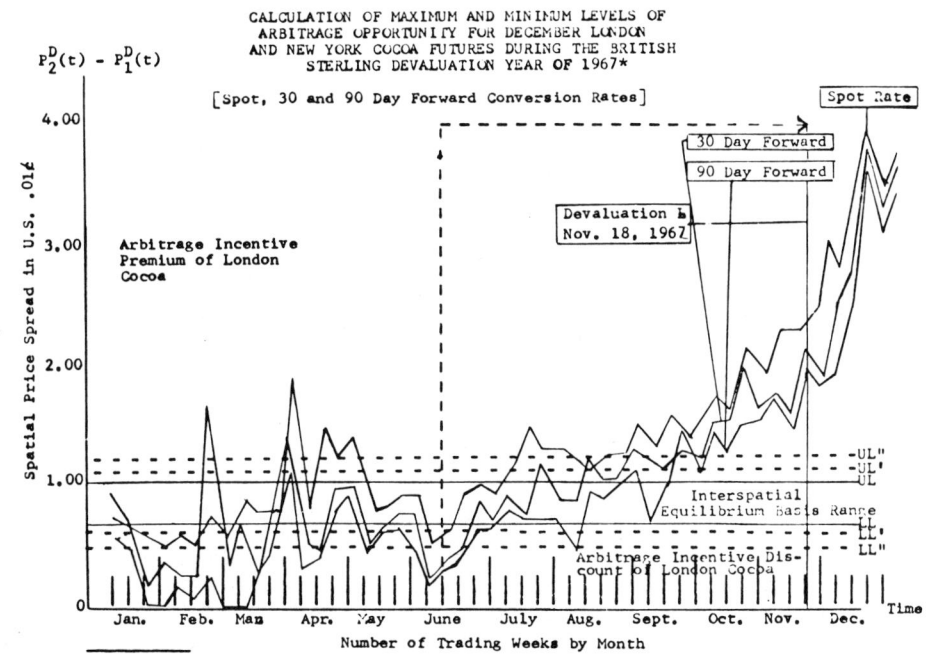

Figure 3-7.

markets, then one should not expect a persistent deviation of the actual from the equilibrium basis. Any spread deviations arising from market disturbances should automatically set into motion the self-correcting forces of arbitrageurs who seek to capitalize on what they consider to be a temporary disparity in the price spread between London and New York futures. Here attempts of arbitrageurs to capitalize on random profits induce other arbitrageurs to enter the market until finally the actual spread tends to equate the equilibrium basis.

Under these conditions, the differing of the actual spread from the equilibrium spread can generally be attributed to the market transactions of non-arbitrageurs. However, the distinction between arbitrageurs and non-arbitrageurs only holds true so long as spread deviations are seen as independent of devaluation expectations. When this assumption is removed, then the distinction between arbitrageurs and nonarbitrageurs loses its reliability.

When devaluation expectations are being harbored by individuals who trade in either of the two cocoa exchanges, New York or London, considerations must be given to possible changes in the real value of cocoa stock holdings resulting from possible revisions in the pound/dollar exchange rate. In circumstances in which individuals expect that official changes in the pound/dollar exchange rate will alter the relative prices between London and New York, then individuals who would normally trade only in domestic futures or limit their transactions in cocoa futures to one exchange would now find that to hedge against changes in the real value of their liquid assets or the real purchasing power of the currency holdings, they must engage in arbitrage transactions between New York and London.

These indirect relative price changes affect the real monetary value of a cocoa futures contract as well as the real value of cocoa stock holdings. For instance, cocoa processors and importers who hold large inventories of cocoa may suddenly find that the value of their stock in terms of British currency has appreciated significantly if the price of foreign exchange has increased. Since cocoa is a commodity that is imported into the United States and the United Kingdom, or reexported between both the United States and the United Kingdom, cocoa buyers and sellers either for immediate or deferred delivery have to be cognizant of possible alterations in the pound/dollar exchange rate. Furthermore, they must also have the economic incentive to time their transactions to take advantage of future exchange rate changes. The existence of a forward exchange facility provides the necessary insurance for hedging against the exchange risk associated with external payments from abroad for cocoa purchases or for the receipt of payments from abroad for cocoa reexports. Nevertheless, "the availability of forward facilities does not solve the problem of choosing the most favorable time to make the exchange commitment."[16]

During a period of devaluation expectations and the resulting absence of a clear distinction between arbitrage and non-arbitrage forces, any compounded deviation of the actual spread from the assumed equilibrium basis must be the outcome of joint market trading. This trading assumes that the equilibrium basis of the future will differ from the current equilibrium basis. Arbitrage transactions that cause a sudden increase in the deviation of the actual spread from the equilibrium basis may be caused by arbitrageurs with one set of expectations about the future equilibrium spread.

Arbitrage activity that tends to cause the actual spread to stop and start in its deviational behavior may be attributed to difference in lag time among arbitrageurs. For example, the arbitrageur may not initiate an arbitrage position immediately following an increase in the actual spread deviation from the current equilibrium basis. He may first wish to satisfy himself that the increase will be sustained for more than one period before he develops his expectations as to whether the actual spread deviation will be moving in the future towards a new equilibrium value or its old one. The required actual spread adjustment will not be achieved instantaneously, and thus changes in the actual spread will be distributed over a number of periods until they reach their new equilibrium level.

Accordingly, this type of market behavior by arbitrageurs might be associated with Cagan's adaptive expectations hypothesis, in which the expected value of the price spread between London and New York is revised per period of time in proportion to the difference between the actual spread value and the value previously expected.

Furthermore, the reason that proportional comparisons are being made between actual and expected spread values stems from the fact that arbitrageurs are formulating strategies based on devaluation expectations. In this case, devaluation expectations are formulated on the basis of evidence that is considered indicative of a country's external disequilibrium.

Variables Influencing Devaluation Expectations

Examples of such evidence might be the corrective measures taken by British monetary authorities who actively enter into the foreign exchange market to stabilize the value of the pound or to curtail losses in their reverse balances. Other examples might be intergovernmental transactions and arrangements among central banks, tax disincentives affecting private capital movements, regulations requiring discrimination in interest rates payable on foreign and domestic accounts, swap agreements between central banks and commercial banks, and restrictions on prohibitions of capital exports and certain types of imports of goods and services. In resorting to measures of this sort, a government implicitly recognizes that the official exchange rate overvalues its currency. Moreover, the greater the restrictive measures relative to a given balance of payments deficit, the greater apparently the degree of overvaluation or of fundamental disequilibrium calling forth exchange rate adjustment. Thus, the problems of trying to estimate the time or the magnitude of an exchange devaluation would be closely linked to a currency's overvaluation.[17]

In the same spirit, it is also possible that a sterling crisis of confidence may arise from an intangible phenomenon. A clear example of this would be the devaluation stigma traditionally attached to the Labor party. One writer has described this difficulty the Labor party seems to have in dissociating itself from blame when the need arises for unorthodox remedies, particularly in the field of finance. He alleged that when Conservatives must act, as in devaluation, they are believed to have been left no option, whereas the same charitableness is not extended to Labor.[18] Because of the existence of an array of tangible and intangible variables that can work in combination to influence devaluation expectations, other things being equal, expected equilibrium spreads will vary with changes in the level of devaluation expectations. Thus, during periods of uncertainty surrounding the parity value of sterling, there may be many expected equilibrium spreads between London and New York. Each set of governmental corrective measures for controlling currency overvaluation may be associated with a particular expected equilibrium basis spread, and to the extent that arbitrageurs are cognizant of the influence of changes in governmental policy, they will tend to initiate an arbitrage position consistent with their expectations of devaluation.

Devaluation Expectations and Arbitrage

This leads us to two additional questions. One, how extensive do deviations between spreads have to be before arbitrage activities of one type counterbalance or dominate the spread movement? And, two, how do you separate those arbitrage transactions that are motivated solely by the quest for arbitrage profits and those initiated as a hedging device against losses in currency or asset purchasing power?

Arbitrage transactions of cocoa traders who seek a hedge against devaluation may result in a dampening or amplifying of the spread deviations that stem from the arbitrage transactions of those who are seeking arbitrage profits. When the price of cocoa futures is not assumed to be independent of changes in the price of foreign exchange, then the spread between London and New York is a function of changes in the pound/dollar exchange rate. Consequently, increases in the price of foreign exchange will tend to raise British cocoa prices because cocoa imports or cocoa futures in New York will cost more. Furthermore, upward pressure on London cocoa futures from any given change in the pound/dollar rate will vary according to devaluation expectations. This has been clearly documented in one of the British business journals, the *Economist,* where a columnist states:

Currency fears have recently been adding fuel to commodity investment, though the results have not always been predictable. . . . In the past six to twelve months, the big action has been in sugar, cocoa, and copper. . . . When the three-month forward rate of sterling stood at four per cent discount on the spot price, it represented a fifty-six pound price differential to tin dealers.[19]

Interspatial Effects of Devaluation on Cocoa Futures

What appears to be evident from Figures 3–8 and 3–9 is that as expectations were developing concerning the devaluation of the pound, the tendency was to buy in London and sell in New York.

One explanation of why people were selling New York and buying London at the onset of the pound sterling pre-devaluation crisis period is that they expected that the price of cocoa would be higher in the future due to the pound/dollar exchange revision brought about by the devaluation of the pound. This explanation seems reasonable since the actual London/New York price spread both in September and December cocoa futures was steadily growing in its premium deviation from the interspatial equilibrium basis range of 75 to 100. If arbitrageurs had not expected an upward shift in the equilibrium basis range, then they would have had to be plying their trade by buying New York and selling London when the price of a delivery contract went to 100 points above the price of a comparable position in New York. But what actually happened was that as the London premium of cocoa increased, arbitrageurs behaved as though they were in a discount market for London cocoa. And as previously argued, for a spread to keep growing outside of the upper limit of its equilibrium basis range, arbitrageurs must foresee a continuous shift of the basis range from the current actual deviation spread, the expectation of British devaluation causing the shift. This does, however, seem to imply that similar supply and demand conditions must be present in both markets, and that any persistent spread deviation increase between the London and New York cocoa exchanges must be due to the devaluation expectations rather than local demand and supply conditions. Perhaps this is overemphasizing the impact of devaluation on cocoa futures but if we examine closely the 1967 time series illustrated in Figures 3–8 and 3–9, which depict price movement comparisons between London and New York December and September cocoa futures, we see an almost identical price trend. The only apparent difference between the London and New York prices is the widening of the interspatial price spread. This similarity in price profile probably results from the fact that "the price trend of cocoa as traded in New York mirrors largely the prior market action that stems from trading which takes place on the London Terminal market. . . ."[20] This evidence has led the author to conclude that any cleavage between the price trend in New York and that in London can be attributed to the influence of devaluation expectation.

COMPARISONS IN PRICE MOVEMENTS BETWEEN LONDON
AND NEW YORK SEPTEMBER COCOA FUTURES DURING
THE BRITISH STERLING DEVALUATION YEAR 1967

[30 Day Forward Currency Conversion Rate]

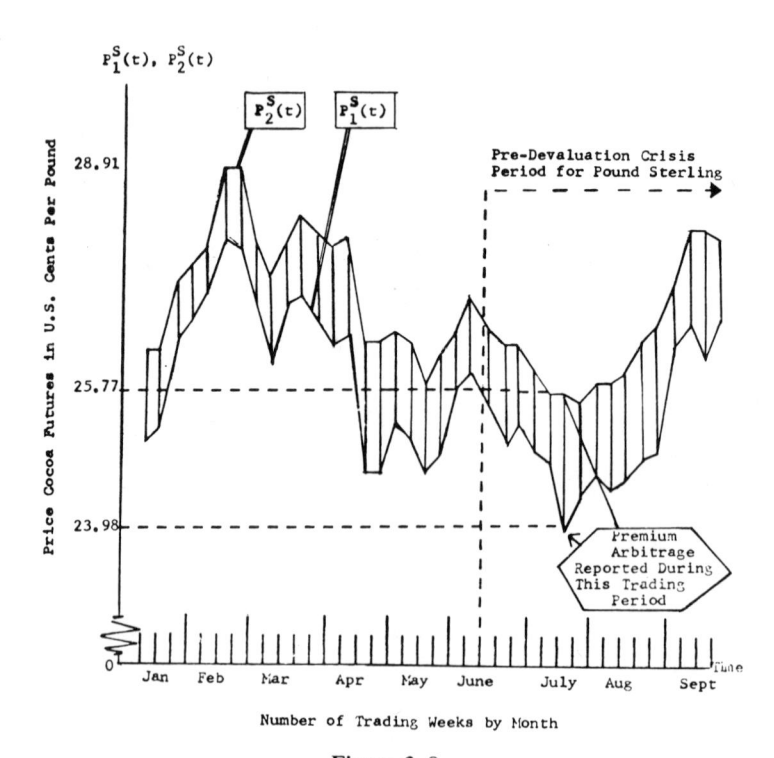

Figure 3-8.

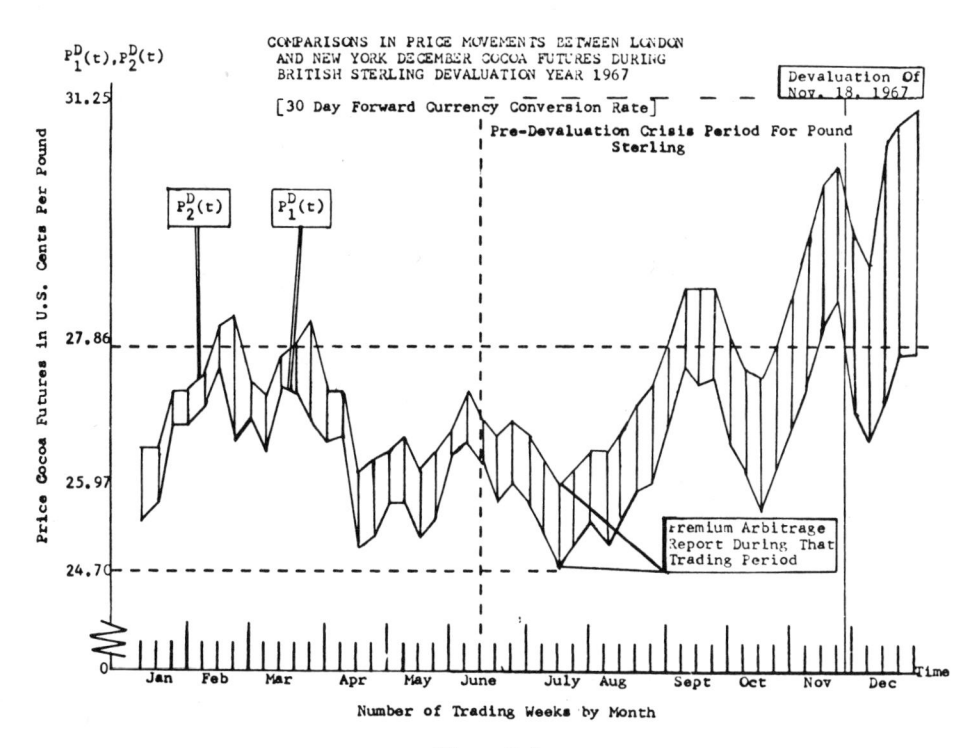

Figure 3-9.

Arbitrage Opportunities during Sterling Devaluation

The continuous widening of the London/New York spread can also be seen in Figures 3–10 and 3–11, which show the arbitrage opportunity between September futures and December futures during the British devaluation year of 1967. In these two diagrams that separately depict the spread movement of September futures and December futures we see at one glance what is happening in the London/New York cocoa market and the pound/dollar foreign exchange market. By converting the price of London futures from shillings to cents through the use of the U.K./U.S. parity exchange rate and the 30-day forward rate, we can compare the widening of interspatial spread with the pound/dollar exchange widening. The September and December diagrams also clearly show that as the differential between the parity rate and the 30-day forward rate began to widen, the interspatial spread also began to widen and to move steadily into the premium arbitrage region. This appreciable inclination towards the premium region can probably best be seen in the December diagram.

Prior to the twenty-three trading periods, when the arbitrage spread went beyond the equilibrium basis, it generally showed a tendency to return to the equilibrium basis. This behavior might be explained by interpreting the arbitrage spread as indication that arbitrageurs did not expect the equilibrium basis to change. And as the arbitrage basis moved outside the equilibrium basis range (upper limit), the expectation was that the arbitrage spread would return to some point within the equilibrium range. This can be seen by the oscillation that took place in and out of the equilibrium basis of 75–100 points. However, after the twenty-third week, the arbitrage spread began to grow further away from the equilibrium basis. This type of spread behavior can be explained in the light of trading expectations that foresaw a change in the equilibrium basis. If the spread between London and New York goes beyond 100 points, the typical behavior is for arbitrageurs to sell London and buy New York simultaneously at time t, with the expectations of buying in London at a lower price and selling in New York at a higher price.

Another interesting observation concerning the effects devaluation expectation can have on the interspatial spread over time may be seen in Figure 3–12, which tries to associate spread movements with political disturbances.[21]

Another reason for expecting a shift in the equilibrium spread between London and New York is that "in two competitive markets separated by space, the prices for the same good may differ but are subject to the constraint

$$-T'_{21}(t) \leqslant P'_2(t) - P'_1(t) \leqslant T'_{12}(t),$$

where $T'_{12}(t)$ represents the transport cost from market 1 [New York] to market 2 [London] and $T'_{21}(t)$ represents the similar transport cost per unit of the goods shipped from market 2 [London] to market 1 [New York].

ARBITRAGE OPPORTUNITIES OF SEPTEMBER FUTURES BETWEEN
LONDON AND NEW YORK COCOA EXCHANGES DURING THE BRITISH
STERLING DEVALUATION YEAR OF 1967*

[Par Value and 30 Day Forward Currency Conversion Rates]

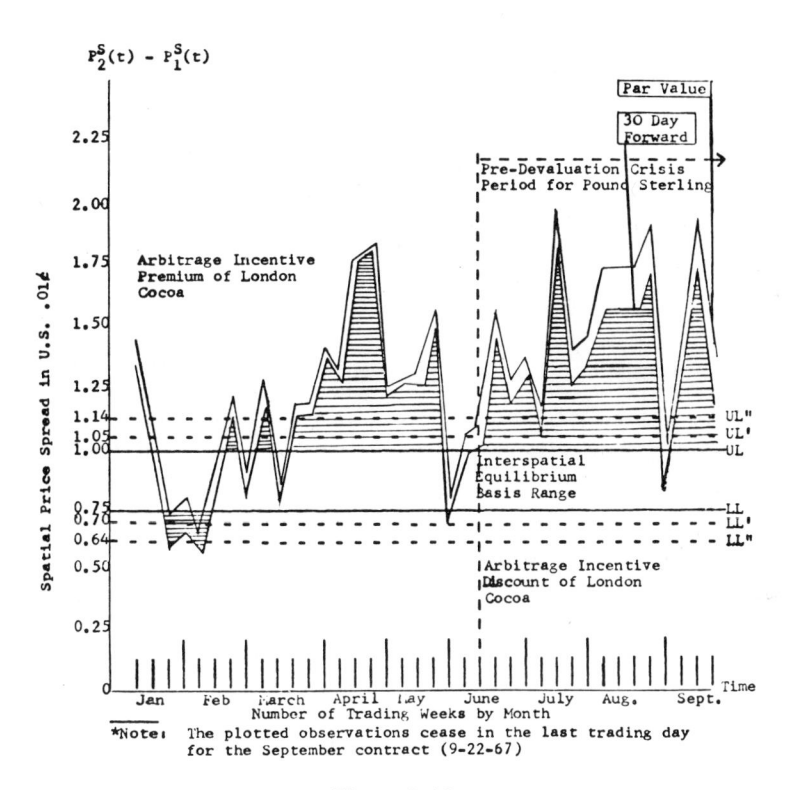

Figure 3-10.

*Note: The plotted observations cease in the last trading day for the September contract (9-22-67)

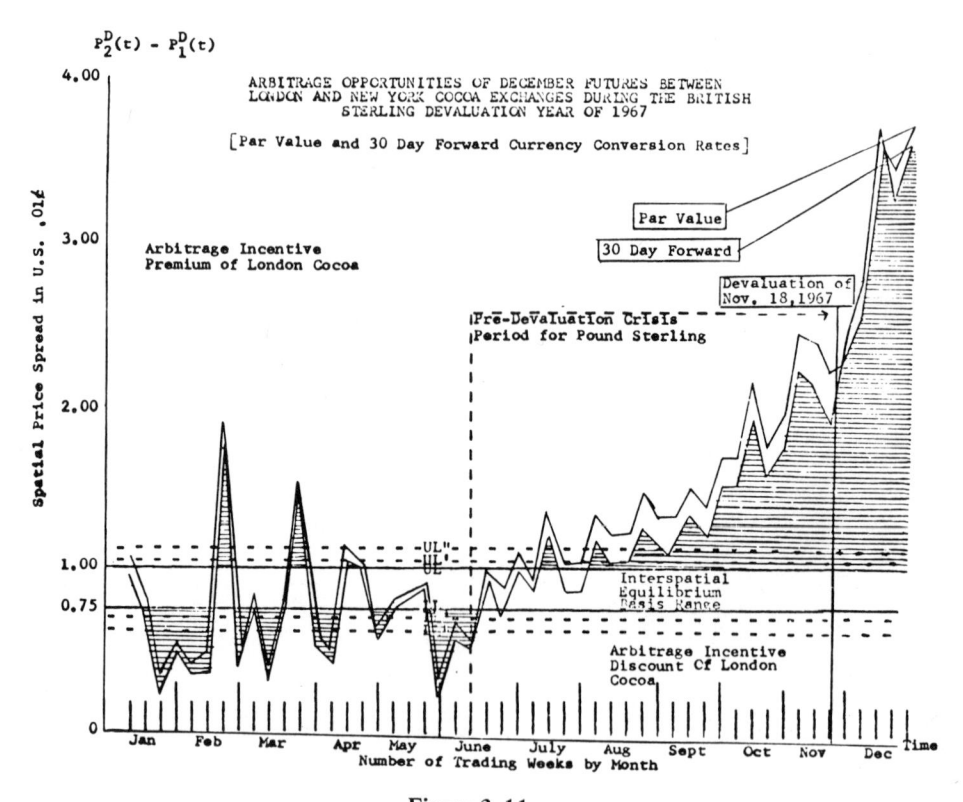

Figure 3-11.

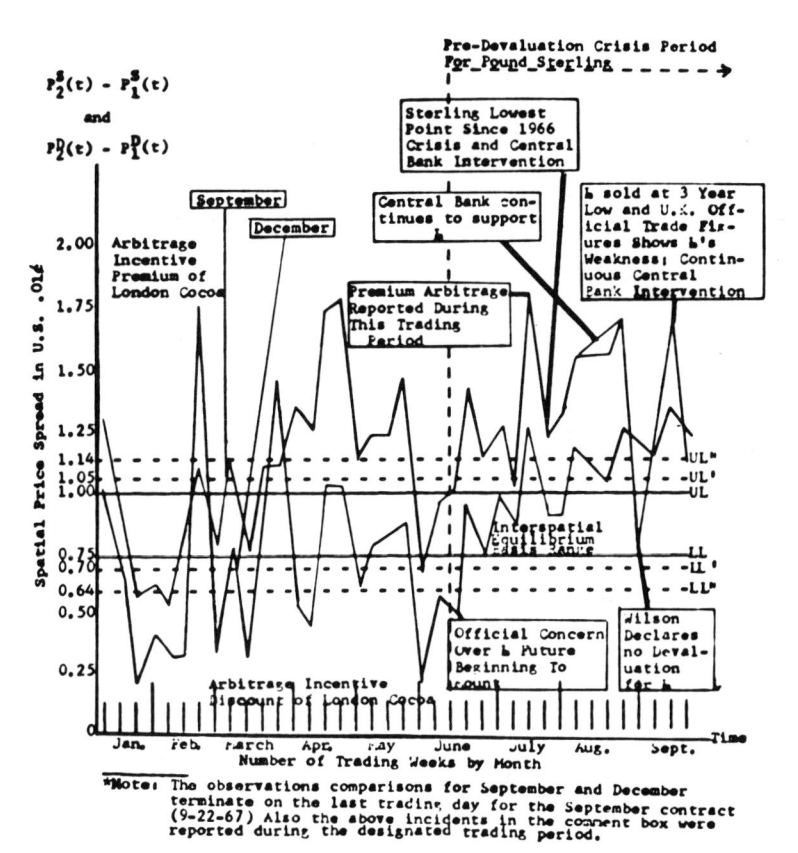

Figure 3-12.

These transport costs consist of freight, insurance, interest in capital tied up in transit, etc."[22]

By using the above relationship, we can also add another explanation of why devaluation expectations lead to the anticipated shift in the equilibrium basis. Arbitrageurs expect devaluation to increase the cost of freight, insurance, and interest related to shipping cocoa from London to New York, or the "round turn" buying and selling foreign commissions cost associated with futures trading, for example $T'_{21}(t+k) > T'_{21}(t)$. These are costs that are external to Great Britain. One journal, in reviewing transport costs on the occasion of devaluation of the pound, described how the international airlines and steamship fare-setting associations would react by raising westbound fares.[23]

Other things being equal, this equilibrium spread between London and New York will differ with realized changes in transport, insurance, and finance cost, but it will also differ from the expectation of costs shifting upward from a realized currency devaluation. And since devaluation expectations may vary during a given period from an expected value approaching zero or one, the closer devaluation expectations approach unity, the more we should expect the actual spread to deviate from the previously accepted equilibrium spread.

Thus various equilibrium spreads between London and New York exist, depending on whether devaluation expectations are changing over time or whether the actual deviated spread is equal to the future expected spread. If the actual spread that deviates from the previously considered equilibrium basis does represent the future expected equilibrium spread, then the actual spread should cease to grow.

The French Devaluation

An incidental point that is of interest is that a currency devaluation from a neighboring country can also have an impact on arbitrage activities between London and New York. The following, from a *Market Letter* published by Rittenhouse Investments, Inc., will illustrate:

August 15, 1967: (New York)—This international commodity [cocoa] responded according to Hoyle following the announcement of the French devaluation. Keen students of market tactics made their operations felt by buying London and selling New York. On Monday, even though the New York market was calculated to be due some 20–30 points higher, it opened sharply lower and continued since the balance of the week, closing near lows on Thursday, August 14.[24]

Two other market letters published in subsequent weeks by B. J. Lind and Company reported a drop in price in New York of cocoa futures in response to devaluation of the franc, and an upsurge in buying of sugar and cocoa in London.[25]

4

Sterling Crisis Periods: Their Price Effects on Futures Markets

The sterling crisis periods to be examined span a ten-year period.[1] This decade, consisting of the crisis peak periods of September 1957, July 1961, November–December 1964, July–August 1965, and July–September 1966, was chosen as the crisis survey sample for two reasons: (1) Data were readily available for both London and New York cocoa exchanges, and (2) the pound was not devalued during these crises. This chapter, then, will discuss why the author chose to examine non-devaluation periods.

Non-Devaluation Sterling Crisis Periods

In Chapter 3, the hypothesis presented to explain the steadily increasing premium spread deviation was that arbitrageurs held devaluation expectations such that they anticipated an upward shift in the London/New York equilibrium basis. To determine if this type of interspatial spread activity can be associated with devaluation expectations, a similar examination was conducted of crises in which devaluation was not realized.

In examining the crises, or "false devaluation periods," methods similar to those described in Chapter 3 were used. Time series were constructed from Friday weekly data of London and New York September and December cocoa futures. The time span for the sample was shortened from twelve months to five months for the 1957 and 1961 crisis periods and to six months for the 1964, 1965, and 1966 crises. The reason for varying the number of observations per crisis is that each crisis peak period was centered between two months prior to the peak of the crisis and two months after. Actual spread deviations from the equilibrium basis range will compound their premium growth if devaluation expectations are present.

Consequently, we concluded that if this type of behavior prevailed during a given crisis period, it would be easily distinguishable from an expected non-unidirectional spread behavior during the precrisis and postcrisis peak periods. It can probably be easily argued that the two-month time span before and after the peak of the crises should have been extended to include additional observations. However, to avoid an inundation of data entries, the decision was made to limit the observation sample to five- and six-month periods. If a twelve-month observation sample had been maintained, the data entries would have easily approached ten thousand entries. Furthermore, since the length of the crisis peak never exceeded more than three months, it seemed appropriate to limit outside observation to two months prior to the peak period and two months after. When the length of the crisis peak period was one month, the sample was limited to five months, and when the crisis period was an interval of two months, the sample period was extended to six months.

The Sterling Crisis of 1957

The first crisis examined is the 1957 September peak crisis, which was characterized by a gold and dollar reserve drain of approximately $700 million, and a net reserve level of $1850 million against an atmosphere of speculation based on the devaluation of the French franc and expectations of revaluation of the German mark.[2] Figures 4–1 and 4–2 indicate that during the 1957 sterling crisis period the market tendency was to buy in London and sell in New York, as the differential between the pound/dollar parity rate and the 30-day forward rates begins to widen. In Figure 4–1, we see that in early July, the actual spread between London and New York was in the discount arbitrage incentive region. We can also see the differential between the par value and the 30-day forward rate, by focusing our attention on the shilling/cent converted spread trend lines. As the gap between the parity and 30-day forward converted differential grows, the interspatial spread deviation in the premium arbitrage region tends to grow. Allowing for slight differences in time series, the 1957 crisis period as seen in Figures 4–1 and 4–2 does seem to go hand in hand with the premium deviational growth of 1967, conveying expectations of an upward shift in the equilibrium basis.[3]

The Sterling Crisis of 1961

Figures 4–3 and 4–4, which represent the arbitrage opportunities of September and December that existed during the 1961 sterling crisis period, do not support the contentions of an expected change in the equilibrium basis range during this British crisis of confidence. The main reason for this contrast between the interspatial spread behavior of 1967 and that of 1961 is that devaluation expectations were not present during this crisis period. The *London Financial Times,* the *Journal of Commerce,* and various periodicals and daily newspapers were examined for the 1961 observation sample period, and there was no clear evidence of devaluation expectations.

The absence of devaluation expectations during this crisis might be attributed to the fact that the Conservatives were in office, and the stigma of devaluation is typically not associated with the Conservative party. Another possible explanation in the same vein is that previous devaluations had not taken place during the month of July.

Apparently, during the crisis periods, the commodity and foreign exchange groups were more concerned about the possibility of a financial adjustment, such as a change in the British bank rate, than about a revision

ARBITRAGE OPPORTUNITIES OF SEPTEMBER FUTURES BETWEEN
LONDON AND NEW YORK COCOA EXCHANGES DURING SEPTEMBER
CRISIS PEAK PERIOD OF 1957 FOR BRITISH STERLING

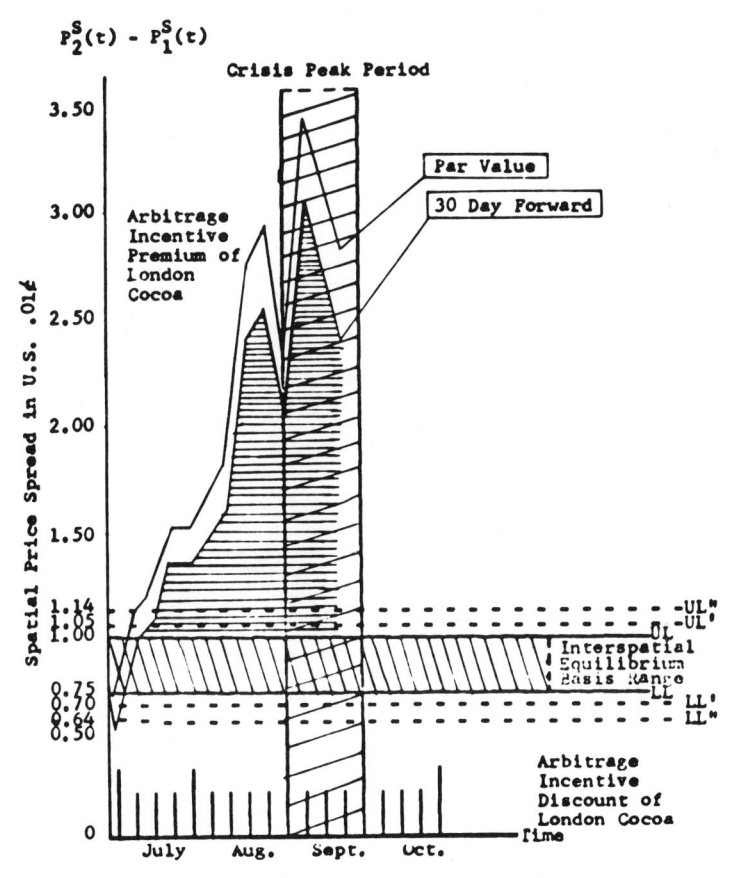

[Par Value and 30 Day Forward Currency Conversion Rates]

Figure 4-1.

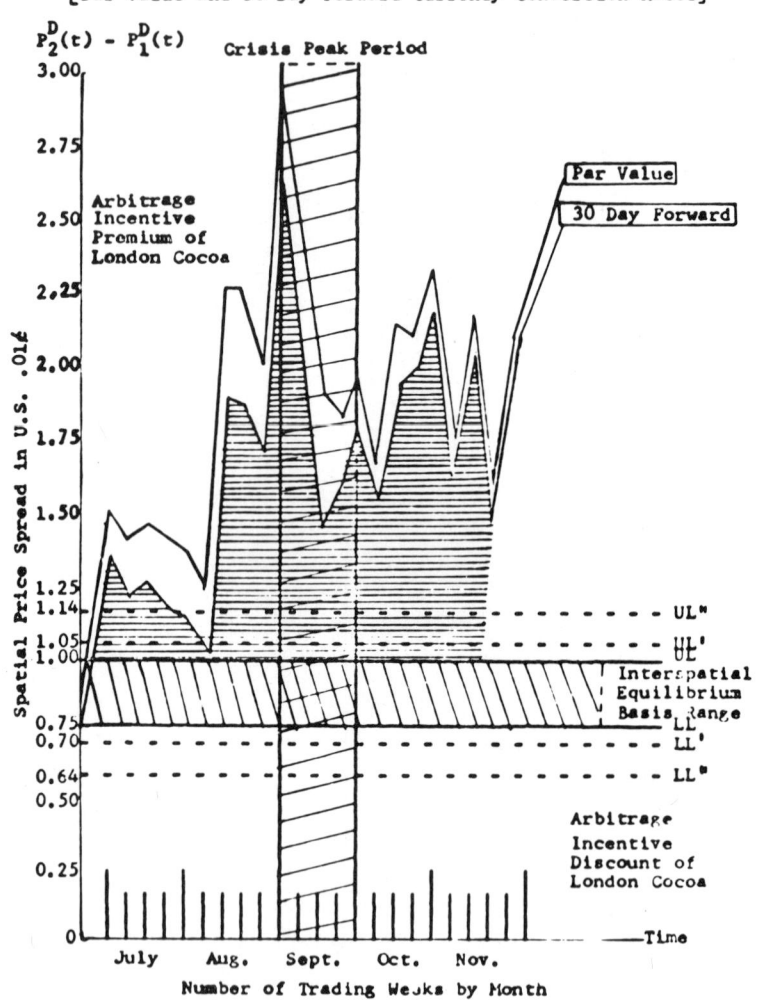

Figure 4-2.

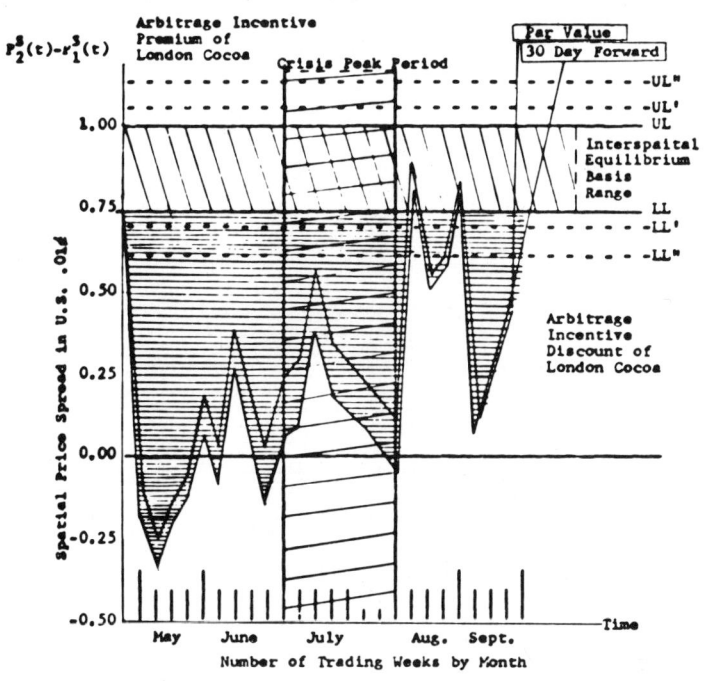

Figure 4-3.

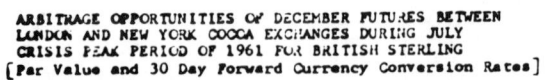

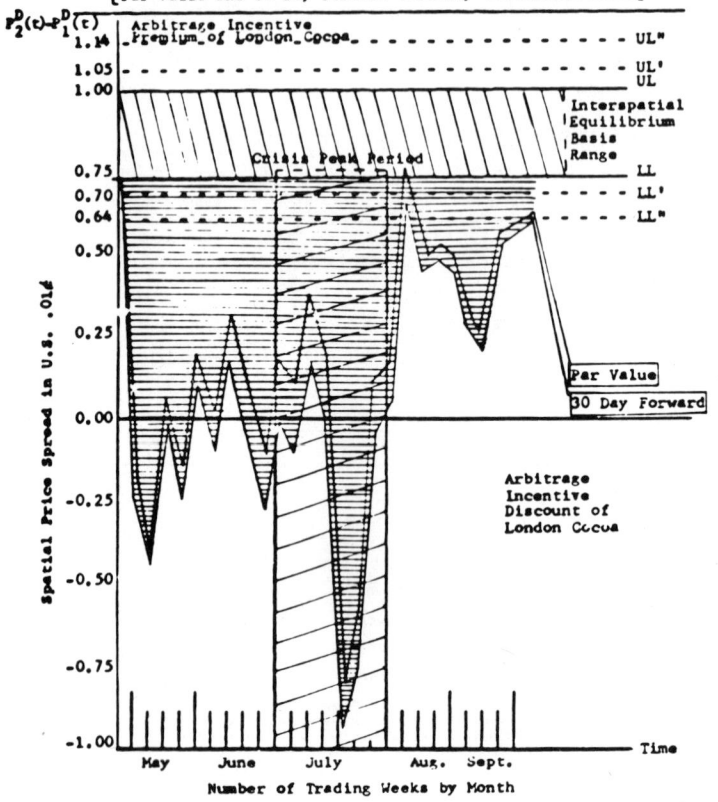

Figure 4-4.

of the pound/dollar rate. The reason for concern among commodity traders was that if the bank rate was increased, the financing of inventory holdings and of new cocoa purchases would be more costly. Thus, during the 1961 crisis, the well-informed arbitrageur quite possibly focused his speculations on the alteration of the British bank rate and on additional alternative fiscal and monetary corrective measures.

Further reasons why corrective measures other than devaluation might be expected are based on the fact that early in July, Parliament was discussing proposals for a finance bill with steps to relieve the pressures on the pound. The measures that the Finance Bill of 1961 would have authorized were (1) a tax ranging up to 10% on the purchase of consumer goods; (2) an increase in the bank rate above its then-current level of 5%; (3) a payroll tax on manpower in industries for which labor was not being fully utilized; (4) an increase in reserve requirements of commercial banks; (5) a reduction of government expenditures both abroad and at home; and (6) governmental efforts to make British goods more competitive abroad. As one journalist observed during the July crisis peak period:

Only last Saturday, in fact, the Treasury Chief Selwyn Lloyd warned the country that it should expect action that would result in a tougher and more competitive spirit in industry, a more critical attitude towards cost, whatever their origin, a relentless rooting out of all inefficiency, restrictiveness and waste, whether it be of capital resources or of labor.[4]

The British Council on Price and Productivity was also drawing the public's attention to the need for productivity improvements. During this same period, the International Monetary Fund announced that it would extend to the British a two-billion-dollar credit to ease Great Britain's balance of payments problems. The I.M.F. also made it known that a comparable sum in standby credits would be available if needed. All in all, most public and official attention was devoted to measures other than devaluation for correcting the 1961 sterling crisis.

There are various explanations of why the sterling crisis year of 1961 demonstrated a discounted spread beween London and New York.[5] If we accept the assumption that futures prices are closely linked between London and New York, and that random supply and demand disturbances generally will show up in both markets concurrently, then we must ask ourselves if explanations outside of market considerations could account for the growing discount divergence between the London/New York actual spread and the equilibrium basis range.

It is conceivable that if the combination of all six corrective measures were expected to be realized, demand for cocoa futures in London could have been driven down to the point where their absolute price value was less than New York's. This would mean that those having bearish expectations visualized a 10% tax being levied on the purchase of cocoa products, thus causing consumers to cut back on their purchases; the increase in the bank rate would force manufacturers and processors of cocoa products to reduce their inventory holdings; the payroll tax would reduce disposable income, thus causing a reduction in overall consumption in those industries where surplus featherbedding might exist; the increase in commercial banks reserve requirement would lead to tighter money conditions, which would add to the liquidity strain to finance cocoa inventories; and finally the reduction of government expenditures could be expected to have indirect adverse effects on aggregate consumption, which would first be felt by nonessentials such as cocoa liquors, chocolate, and so forth. At this point, it is necessary to state that these conclusions derived from observing the 1961 crisis period are inevitably tentative, and given the techniques used in this type of investigation, it is not possible to strongly ascertain what caused the discount spread divergence between London and New York.

The historical narrative that follows is intended to be a brief chronology of the 1961 sterling crisis.

May 29, 1961: *World Money Front*: Once again the pound sterling was subject to continental selling pressure at the end of the week, the British currency falling $2.7917. . . . Traders here reported that the pound was sold quite heavily in the London Market . . . sterling fell to a low for the current downturn, dropping to the lowest point since September 1957.[6]

June 19, 1961: *World Money Front*: Before the market opened here [New York], the British currency had weakened sharply against trading Continental currencies. . . . In the afternoon it was quoted at $2.78 29/32, the *lowest level* reached since September 1957.[7]

July 10, 1961: *World Money Front*: Now with weakness in the U.K.'s payments leading to persistent heavy pressure on regular sterling—external account used to finance current transactions—it is felt that Britain must soon announce fiscal or monetary measures to cope with the situation. In foreign exchange circles, many think this will include a sharp *rise* in the *bank rate* from its present level of 5 per cent. This expectation, traders noted on Friday, is also tending to widen the discount on forwards that currently is around 4 1/3 per cent per annum.[8]

July 25, 1961: *World Money Front*: Prior to the announcement of the tight money–high interest rate program by the Chancellor of the Exchequer yesterday, the pound sterling had eased slightly. It immediately *firmed* with some buying reported from the Continent on news that the *bank rate* was to be *hiked* from 5 to 7 per cent. A much more active trading session is expected by some operators today since they anticipate that German and Swiss interest that have been *short* on Sterling may *decide to cover*.[9]

July 26, 1961: *World Money Front*: The pound sterling opened higher and was traded fairly actively in the morning reportedly because of Continental's *covering of short positions*.[10]

July 26, 1961: *Commodity Futures*: The London bank rate rise would make *financing* of [cocoa] inventories *more expensive* [and consequently] further softened [cocoa] prices.[11]

September 8, 1961: *World Money Front*: The pound sterling that ran up a [half-cent] in European markets last Monday-Tuesday following publication of the end of August reserves figures fluctuated within a rather narrow range in the latter part of the week in a thin market. At one time in Friday's session here [New York], however, the pound slipped below $2.81, reportedly largely because of German selling.[12]

The Sterling Crisis of 1964

The September futures situation is not included in the examination of the 1964 crisis period because the terminal date in September permitted only four observations during the sample period.

As can be seen in Figure 4–5, there appears to be no evidence that spread deviations were reflecting devaluation expectations. If a one-directional growing premium spread deviation can rightfully serve to represent devaluation expectations, then it is apparent from looking at Figure 4–5 that both the 30-day and parity converted spreads remained fairly much within the equilibrium basis range, reflecting zero devaluation expectations. If people harbored devaluation expectations before or at the time of Wilson's election to Parliament, these expectations did not manifest themselves in the behavior of the interspatial spread even though the gap between parity and the 30-day forward rate were sizeable before and all through the crisis period.

Moreover, the only sharp deviation from the equilibrium basis took place before the crisis peak period, and it was in the discount arbitrage range. This situation is peculiar since the daily periodical did cite rumors of devaluation of the pound during the 1964 crisis. However, these rumors were probably discounted by the well-informed arbitrageur because of "the relatively good performance of Britain's gold reserves."[13] Furthermore, Britain was expected to call on its swap agreement with the United States or to take advantage of its billion-dollar standby credit with the International Monetary Fund during this period.

Another significant point is that because of the narrow margin by which Labor had won the Parliamentary elections, the Labor party had too small a mandate to enact a devaluation of the pound. As one source states, "temporarily higher money rates to check movements of uneasy capital possibly fortified by more direct government controls, and an intensified scramble for export markets, appeared to be the most likely sequel to a narrow Labor Party victory in the British elections."[14]

The Sterling Crisis of 1965

As can be seen in Figures 4–6 and 4–7, the interspatial spread behavior between London and New York was distinctly different between September

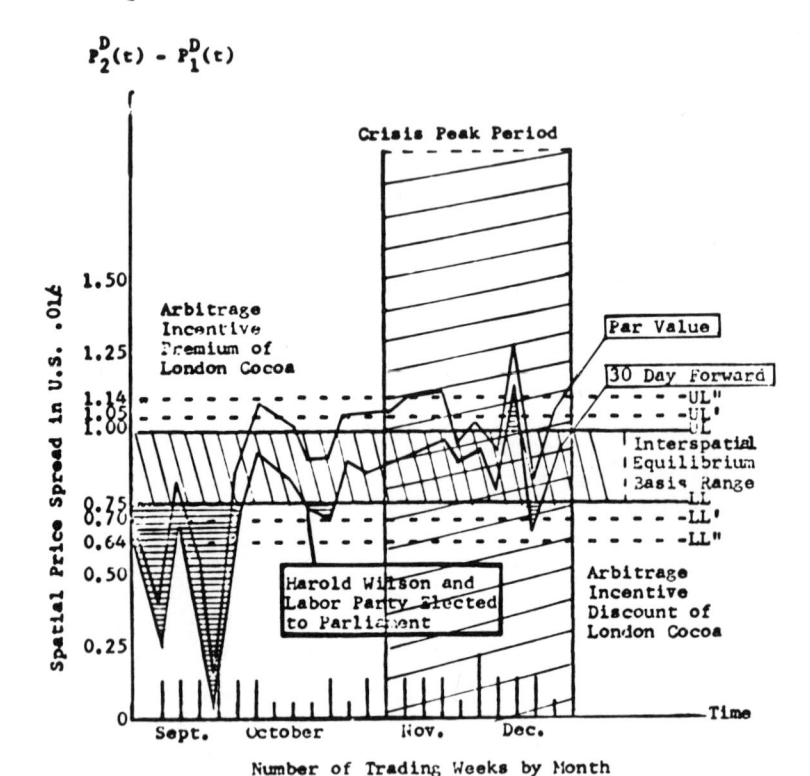

Figure 4-5.

ARBITRAGE OPPORTUNITIES OF SEPTEMBER FUTURES BETWEEN
LONDON AND NEW YORK COCOA EXCHANGES DURING JULY-AUGUST
CRISIS PEAK PERIOD OF 1965 FOR BRITISH STERLING

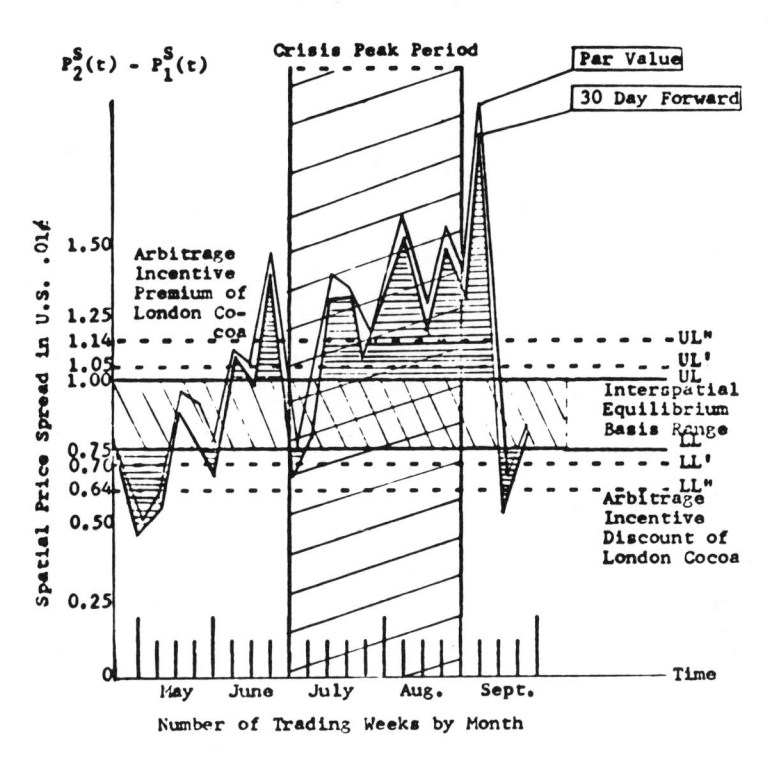

[Par Value and 30 Day Forward Currency Conversion Rates]

Figure 4-6.

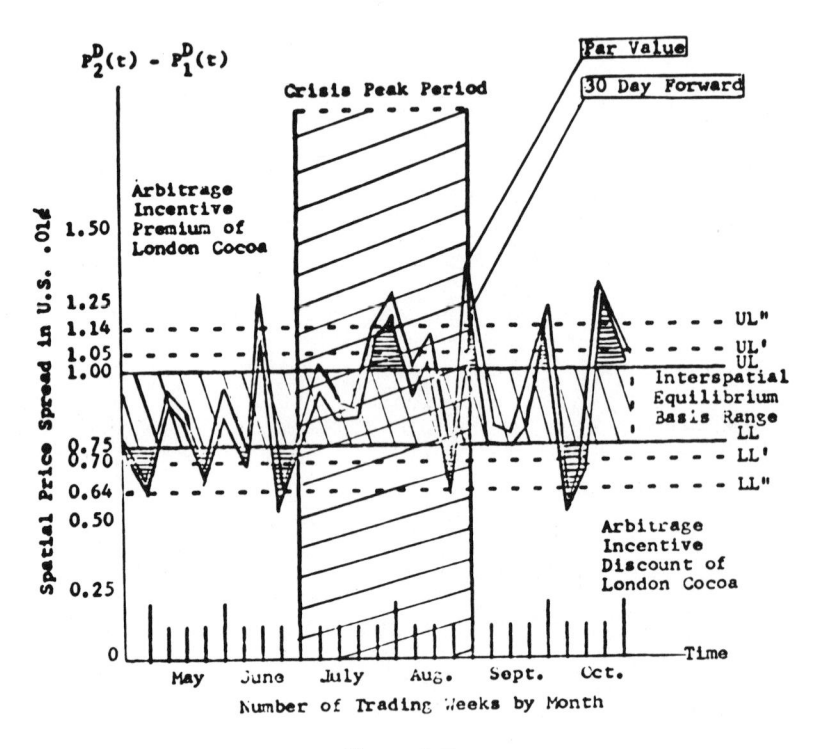

Figure 4-7.

and December futures. December, the more distant month, seemed to move in a pattern very similar to the price trend movement during a non-crisis period, particularly if we impose the maximum (UL'') and minimum (LL'') limits of error. The price trend would in this case be interpreted as moving within its interspatial equilibrium basis range with occasional peaks and troughs intruding into the premium and discount arbitrage regions.

On the other hand, the September spread did display a trend similar to those of the crisis periods of 1957 and 1967. During 1965, the Bank of England's Quarterly Bulletin stated that

> deflation by itself produces only a temporary stimulus for the trade balance, basically through lower imports. To achieve a lasting improvement, manufacturers and traders need to be given a specific incentive to switch resources into the balance of payments. Devaluation does this by increasing the profitability of exports and reducing the profitability of imports.[15]

The following statement is another indication that devaluation expectations were prevalent during the 1965 crisis:

> No one could be certain whether a sterling devaluation would in fact, carry the dollar with it. Certainly, the pressures would be strong. My own guess in mid-1965 is that a devaluation of the pound is likely to carry the dollar down too, with the pound probably dropping significantly more, but both currencies depreciating in relation to the common market currencies.[16]

As an ex-post matter, it is apparent that the above speculation did not materialize, but it serves to verify the existence of devaluation expectations and thus to help to explain September's, if not December's, spread behavior.

The Sterling Crisis of 1966

In examining the spread behavior during the three-month crisis period of 1966, as depicted in Figures 4–8 and 4–9, certain characteristics are apparent.

1. December moves occasionally in and out of equilibrium basis; the general spread stays within the discount arbitrage range until the last crisis month; then the spread begins to move toward the premium arbitrage region, and after the termination of the crisis peak period, it ends up compounding its upward movements into the premium arbitrage region.
2. September enters the crisis period at a premium spread, travels through the equilibrium basis for a couple of trading periods, and then drops into the discount arbitrage zone and remains in this region until the time of its contract maturity.
3. Both December and September tend to oscillate between discount and equilibrium during crisis periods.
4. December oscillates between discount and premium after the crisis peak period and September does so before the crisis period.

ARBITRAGE OPPORTUNITIES OF SEPTEMBER FUTURES BETWEEN
LONDON AND NEW YORK COCOA EXCHANGES DURING JULY-AUGUST-
SEPTEMBER CRISIS PEAK PERIOD OF 1966 FOR BRITISH STERLING

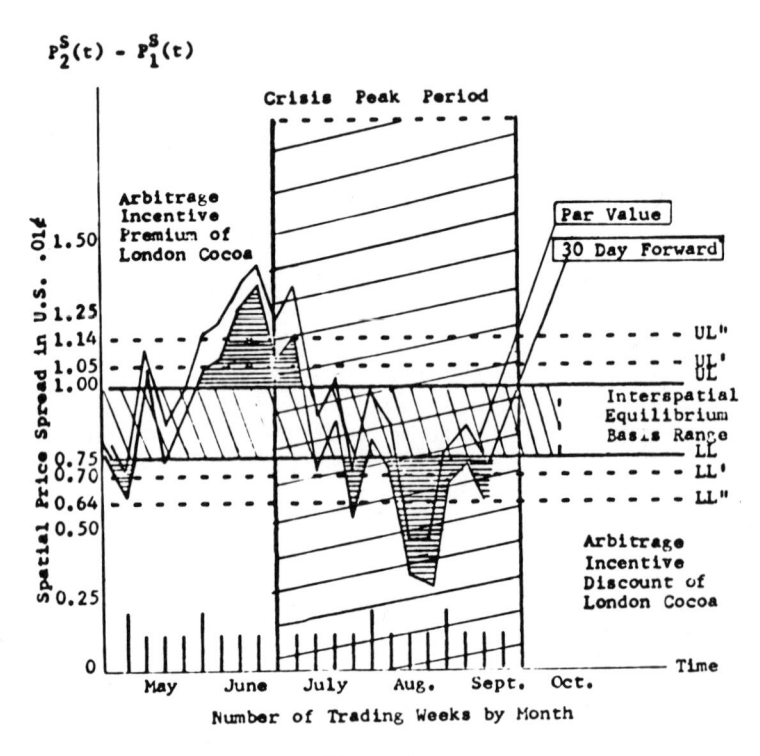

[Par Value and 30 Day Forward Currency Conversion Rates

Figure 4-8.

ARBITRAGE OPPORTUNITIES OF DECEMBER FUTURES BETWEEN LONDON AND NEW YORK COCOA EXCHANGES DURING JULY-AUGUST-SEPTEMBER CRISIS PEAK PERIOD OF 1966 FOR BRITISH STERLING

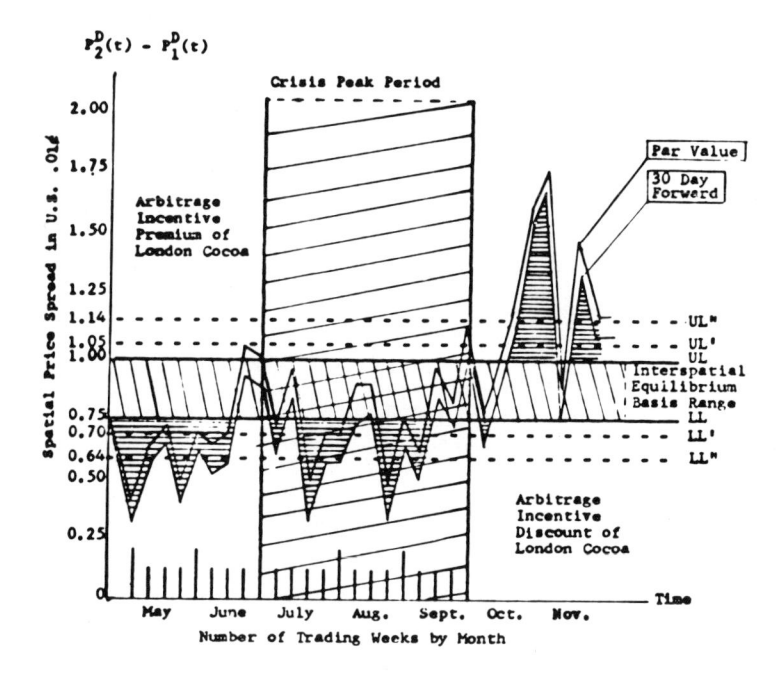

[Par Value and 30 Day Forward Currency Conversion Rates]

Figure 4-9.

An explanation similar to the one offered for the 1961 crisis can also be made for 1966. Namely, that well-informed arbitrageurs did not harbor devaluation expectations, and as the 1966 crisis period developed there was no incentive to buy London and sell New York in the expectation that the price of London would become dearer and the price of New York cheaper. For one thing, during the months of the crisis peak period, foreign exchange groups were pointing to the "good recovery" of the pound; the autonomous behavior between the gold and the foreign exchange market; the firm credit support available to the pound from outside sources; and the general shift in interest from the pound towards other currencies.

This historical narrative of events can be seen in the chronological press statements that follow Figures 4–8 and 4–9.

July 25, 1966: *World Money Front:* After experiencing tumultuous selling in the first three days of last week, the pound scored a *good recovery* as the Wilson government's record austerity program was unfolded. As last week ended, sterling was in a safe haven well above $2.79.[17]

August 15, 1966: *World Money Front:* Nervousness about the longer term outlook for British pounds was a factor bestirring the gold market, was *not* evident in foreign exchange. Sterling was in light supply and in light demand around $2.7894 at the close, which was off slightly from $2.7901 quoted on Thursday which is usually the day of the week when the pound is strongest.[18]

September 16, 1966: *World Money Front:* With the pound more *firmly underpenned* by foreign credits than it has ever been and with signs of improvement in British trade and payments figures, interest in foreign currencies is *veering toward other areas.* Probably of most interest this week will be the trend in some of the Continental European rates. As last week ended, the French franc, under pressure . . . moved fractionally downward to set a *new low* for the last seven years at 20.32½ cents. . . . During the recent recovery in the pound, the Bank of England turned buyer of dollars, which tended to keep the pound from rising further. Pounds on Friday for 90 days futures delivery were at a discount of 58 points from the spot rate.[19]

Concluding Remarks

The principal purpose of this study was to investigate the price effects that devaluation may transmit to two closely related futures markets. Throughout the study the author has sought to explain short-run price behavior during various sterling crisis periods. The conclusions drawn from this study indicate strongly that devaluation does have a unique impact on futures markets. Empirical evidence shows that the futures spread between London and New York does become increasingly responsive to devaluation expectations. Dynamic effects lead concurrently to an upward pressure on the London price and a downward thrust on New York futures.

The several issues that have been raised in this study suggest that the profitability of further research will depend on an investigation of the interrelationship between the term structure of futures and foreign exchange markets that is comparable to studies conducted on interest rates.[20] Many writers have suggested various ways to treat expectations; however, little has been accomplished toward securing an appropriate index for devaluation expectations. Therefore the significance of further research into devaluation's price effects on futures markets will depend largely on a meaningful measure of expectation that takes into account balance of payments variables and commodity trade flows.

Data Appendix

The principal data source used was the *New York Journal of Commerce*. The data entries for London and New York cocoa futures prices and for sterling spot and forward foreign exchange rates were extracted from the microfilm archives at the MIT Dewey Library and the Harvard Business School Baker Library. Other data sources occasionally used were the *Wall Street Journal* and the *British Financial Times*. These sources were consulted when it was believed that a printing error might exist in the data entries of the *Journal of Commerce*.

All data used in Chapter 4 are listed in the data matrix that follows. The data arrangement reads from left to right for each row of entries. The first row and column entry is the observation associated with the first trading week; and in a similar fashion, the first row, second column entry is the observation of the second trading week in the observation sample; and so on.

The data sample for each variable begins by stating the observation interval, the cocoa exchanges to which the observations are relevant, and the delivery month of the futures contract. The variable name and definition of the variables, and when relevant, the foreign exchange conversion rate, are stated on the final line that precedes the data entries. For example, the first variable's data description and listing would read thus:

The data test sample period observed covered the time period from January 6, 1967 to December 21, 1967. The data entries are Friday weekly observations for both the London and New York December cocoa futures. The variable's name is $P_2^D(t)$ where

$$P = \text{price} \qquad D = \text{December} \qquad (t) = \text{time}$$
$$2 = \text{market 2 (London)}$$

which is defined as the London December cocoa futures price and is denominated in U.K. shillings per long hundredweight (cwt). Also, a variable name such as $[A_{ij}^D(t)]_s^l$ would read as follows:

$$A = \text{arbitrage} \qquad D = \text{December} \qquad l = \text{New York's low price}$$
$$(t) = \text{time or trading period}$$
$$ij = \text{market } I \text{ and } J = (1, 2) \text{ and } (2, 1) \qquad s = \text{spot foreign exchange rate}$$

Instead of exact market values of 1 and 2 being assigned to the subscripts of A, i and j were used to indicate that the arbitrage incentive may change throughout the observation sample from A_{12} to A_{21}, each implying different arbitrage incentives. The letter l represents the New York low price used in the calculation of the arbitrage incentive and is used in conjunction with the spot foreign exchange rate s to measure and convert the variable into U.S. value of 0.01 cent.

Data Test Sample Period : 1/6/67-12/21/67
Friday Weekly Observations for London and New York December Data

$P_2^D(t)$: London Dec. Cocoa Futures Price (U.K. Shillings per Cwt):

211.600	212.000	218.000	218.600
220.000	225.000	226.600	219.600
217.600	222.000	223.600	226.000
217.600	218.000	209.000	210.000
211.600	212.000	208.600	211.000
214.000	217.600	214.600	213.600
214.600	214.000	210.600	208.600
210.000	212.000	212.000	213.000
216.000	219.600	224.600	231.000
231.000	231.000	226.000	222.000
221.000	224.000	229.600	236.600
243.000	245.600	272.600	268.600
285.600	290.600	292.600	

$[P_2^D(t)]_v$: London Dec. Cocoa Futures Price (U.S. ¢ Per Lb.)

U.K./U.S. Par Value Currency Conversion Rate:

26.4500	26.5000	27.2500	27.3250
27.5000	28.1250	28.3250	27.4500
27.2000	27.7500	27.9500	28.2500
27.2000	27.2500	26.1250	26.2500
26.4500	26.5000	26.0750	26.3750
26.7500	27.2000	26.8250	26.7000
26.8250	26.7500	26.3250	26.0750
26.2500	26.5000	26.5000	26.6250
27.0000	27.4500	28.0750	28.8750
28.8750	28.8750	28.2500	27.7500
27.6250	28.0000	28.7000	29.5750
30.3750	30.7000	29.2176	28.7888
30.6109	31.1468	31.3612	

$[P_2^D(t)]_s$: London Dec. Cocoa Futures Price (U.S. ¢ Per Lb.)

U.K./U.S. Spot Currency Conversion Rate:

26.3564	26.4101	27.1624	27.2527
27.4538	28.0717	28.2663	27.3774
27.1446	27.7083	27.9140	28.2268
27.1757	27.2383	26.1287	26.2396
26.4386	26.4895	26.0489	26.3316
26.6984	27.1300	26.7541	26.6237
26.7253	26.6544	26.2234	25.9688
26.1243	26.3675	26.3608	26.4776
26.8640	27.2961	27.9306	28.7089
28.7048	28.7007	28.0845	27.5854
27.4523	27.8300	28.5247	29.3891
30.1862	30.5081	29.4505	29.0184
30.6956	31.1473	31.4153	

Data Test Sample Period : 1/6/67-12/21/67

Friday Weekly Observations for London and New York December Data

$[P_2^D(t)]_3$: London Dec. Cocoa Futures Price (U.S. ¢ Per Lb.)

U.K./U.S. 30 Day Forward Currency Conversion Rate:

26.3517	26.3911	27.1429	27.2283
27.4341	28.0506	28.2461	27.3637
27.1281	27.6935	27.9030	28.2076
27.1601	27.2149	26.1091	26.2190
26.4122	26.4754	26.0377	26.3213
26.6879	27.1145	26.7445	26.6170
26.7205	26.6487	26.2253	25.9651
26.1046	26.3618	26.3580	26.4662
26.8524	27.2823	27.9105	28.6945
28.6852	28.6914	28.0684	27.5775
27.4395	27.8080	28.4991	29.3626
30.1406	30.4258	29.4079	28.9848
30.6191	30.9657	31.2533	

$[P_2^D(t)]_6$: London Dec. Cocoa Futures Price (U.S. ¢ Per Lb.)

U.K./U.S. 60 Day Forward Currency Conversion Rate:

26.3385	26.3817	27.1235	27.2166
27.4204	28.0386	28.2359	27.3480
27.1057	27.6707	27.8821	28.1824
27.1407	27.1964	26.0904	26.2021
26.3914	26.4517	26.0163	26.3034
26.6687	27.1009	26.7368	26.6056
26.7263	26.6372	26.2197	25.9539
26.0897	26.3410	26.3381	26.4491
26.8312	27.2617	27.8955	28.6667
28.6636	28.6739	28.0542	27.5547
27.4148	27.7770	28.4785	29.3310
30.1102	30.4258	29.3896	28.9584
30.5553	30.8749	31.1083	

$[P_2^D(t)]_9$: London Dec. Cocoa Futures Price (U.S. ¢ Per Lb.)

U.K./U.S. 90 Day Forward Currency Conversion Rate:

26.3196	26.3646	27.1156	27.2039
27.4008	28.0175	28.2157	27.3274
27.0921	27.6538	27.8661	28.1662
27.1232	27.1779	26.0718	26.1834
26.3744	26.4384	26.0005	26.2855
26.6535	27.0873	26.7234	26.5941
26.6985	26.6258	26.2065	25.9474
26.0756	26.3268	26.3239	26.4357
26.8196	27.2470	27.8795	28.6491
28.6481	28.6512	28.0401	27.5399
27.3990	27.7640	28.4581	29.3098
30.0854	30.3601	29.3653	28.9344
30.5043	30.7971	31.0299	

Data Test Sample Period : 1/6/67-12/21/67

Friday Weekly Observations for London and New York December Data

$[A^D_{ij}(t)]^o_v$: Arbitrage Incentive Dec. Cocoa Futures (U.S. 0.01¢) Using

U.K./U.S. Par Value Currency Conversion Rate & N.Y. Opening Price:

1.10002	0.880020	0.450012	0.625000
0.500000	0.525009	1.82501	0.600021
0.900009	0.490005	0.850006	1.50002
0.670013	0.600021	1.08501	1.09001
0.720001	0.870010	0.925018	0.975006
0.400024	0.740005	0.675018	1.06001
0.915009	1.12001	1.00502	1.37500
1.09001	1.08002	1.35002	1.27502
1.25002	1.45000	1.37500	1.33502
1.52502	1.42502	1.70003	1.70001
2.10503	1.77000	1.96001	2.37500
2.32501	2.18002	2.21756	2.48885
3.52092	3.30684	3.50119	

$[A^D_{ij}(t)]^o_s$: Arbitrage Incentive Dec. Cocoa Futures (U.S. 0.01¢) Using

U.K./U.S. Spot Currency Conversion Rate & N.Y. Opening Price:

1.00647	0.790085	0.362396	0.552750
0.453781	0.471741	1.76630	0.527451
0.844604	0.448334	0.814026	1.47678
0.645691	0.588303	1.08871	1.07965
0.708618	0.859558	0.898911	0.931625
0.348404	0.670029	0.604095	0.983719
0.815338	1.02446	0.903442	1.26880
0.964340	0.947495	1.21085	1.12759
1.11400	1.29605	1.23056	1.16895
1.35481	1.25069	1.53452	1.53545
1.93234	1.59998	1.78470	2.18906
2.13620	1.98811	2.45050	2.71838
3.60559	3.30736	3.55530	

$[A^D_{ij}(t)]^l_s$: Arbitrage Incentive Dec. Cocoa Futures (U.S. 0.01¢) Using

U.K./U.S. Spot Currency Conversion Rate & N.Y. Low Price:

0.826385	0.760101	0.642410	0.602692
0.643784	0.571686	0.766296	0.677368
0.844589	0.808289	0.813995	1.82678
0.845673	1.43829	1.21867	1.35960
0.838593	0.899475	0.928894	0.981598
0.588394	0.669998	0.954086	0.983673
0.915283	1.16438	1.45338	1.30879
1.31428	0.427475	1.18080	1.26758
1.23389	1.41611	1.33060	1.50888
1.38451	1.55070	1.66449	1.61537
1.99228	1.88000	2.14468	2.18906
2.33620	2.78809	2.55048	2.41840
3.74559	3.34727	3.57529	

Data Test Sample Period : 1/6/67-12/21/67
Friday Weekly Observations for London and New York December Data

$[A^D_{ij}(t)]^0_3$: Arbitrage Incentive Dec. Cocoa Futures (U.S. 0.01¢) Using

U.K./U.S. 30 Day Forward Currency Conversion Rate & N.Y. Opening Price:

1.00174	0.771133	0.342941	0.528351
0.434143	0.450653	1.74608	0.513702
0.828094	0.433472	0.803040	1.45760
0.630142	0.564941	1.06909	1.05904
0.682190	0.845367	0.887741	0.921280
0.337875	0.654480	0.594498	0.977005
0.810547	1.01871	0.905319	1.26506
0.944656	0.941788	1.20802	1.11618
1.10245	1.28233	1.21051	1.15453
1.33524	1.24142	1.51840	1.52754
1.91949	1.57799	1.75908	2.16263
2.09064	1.90585	2.40788	2.68480
3.52908	3.12575	3.39333	

$[A^D_{ij}(t)]^0_6$: Arbitrage Incentive Dec. Cocoa Futures (U.S. 0.01¢) Using

U.K./U.S. 60 Day Forward Currency Conversion Rate & N.Y. Opening Price:

0.988510	0.761688	0.323486	0.516632
0.420410	0.438583	1.73595	0.498032
0.805756	0.410706	0.782074	1.43237
0.610718	0.546463	1.05045	1.04216
0.661392	0.821716	0.866302	0.903381
0.318771	0.640884	0.586853	0.965576
0.816299	1.00723	0.899673	1.25392
0.929672	0.920975	1.18816	1.09908
1.08124	1.26175	1.19548	1.12668
1.31358	1.22389	1.50427	1.50475
1.89484	1.54698	1.73856	2.13097
2.06024	1.90585	2.38965	2.65842
3.46533	3.03493	3.24832	

$[A^D_{ij}(t)]^0_9$: Arbitrage Incentive Dec. Cocoa Futures (U.S. 0.01¢) Using

U.K./U.S. 90 Day Forward Currency Conversion Rate & N.Y. Opening Price:

0.969620	0.744629	0.315659	0.503952
0.400772	0.417496	1.71571	0.477448
0.792145	0.393845	0.766113	1.41623
0.593231	0.527969	1.03178	1.02342
0.644424	0.808441	0.850510	0.885498
0.303497	0.627274	0.573425	0.954132
0.788513	0.995804	0.886520	1.24738
0.915588	0.906784	1.17395	1.08577
1.06966	1.24702	1.17946	1.10913
1.29813	1.20119	1.49013	1.48987
1.87906	1.53397	1.71806	2.10985
2.03639	1.84009	2.36531	2.63445
3.41436	2.95708	3.16995	

Data Test Sample Period : 1/6/67-12/21/67

Friday Weekly Observations for London and New York December Data

$[A_{ij}^D(t)]_9^h$: Arbitrage Incentive Dec. Cocoa Futures (U.S. 0.01¢) Using

U.K./U.S. 90 Day Forward Currency Conversion Rate & N.Y. High Prices:

0.649582	0.584595	0.165588	0.153885
0.320801	0.197495	0.395691	0.773773E-01
0.920868E-01	0.353775	0.566086	1.41620
0.453186	0.527878	0.871780	1.01338
0.634384	0.738388	0.750504	0.505478
0.303482	0.447281	0.573395	0.714096
0.758484	0.905777	0.836502	0.837387
0.815582	0.576782	1.00388	0.925690
1.03958	1.12700	0.779465	1.08908
1.44807	1.20119	1.44009	1.33986
1.48898	1.53400	1.71808	1.45979
1.88638	1.84010	1.86528	2.33440
3.41428	2.95709	3.16988	2.33440

$[P_I^D(t)]^o$: N.Y. Dec. Cocoa Futures Opening Price (U.S. ¢ Per Lb.):

25.3500	25.6200	26.8000	26.7000
27.0000	27.6000	26.5000	26.8500
26.3000	27.2600	27.1000	26.7500
26.6500	26.6500	25.0400	25.1600
25.7300	25.6300	25.1500	25.4000
26.3500	26.4600	26.1500	25.6400
25.9100	25.6300	25.3200	24.7000
25.1600	25.4200	25.1500	25.3500
25.7500	26.0000	26.7000	27.5400
27.3500	27.4500	26.5500	26.0500
25.5200	26.2300	26.7400	27.2000
28.0500	28.5200	27.0000	26.3000
27.0900	27.8400	27.8600	

$[P_I^D(t)]^h$: N.Y. Dec. Cocoa Futures High Price (U.S. ¢ Per Lb.):

25.6700	25.7800	26.9500	27.0500
27.0800	27.8200	27.8200	27.2500
27.0000	27.3000	27.3000	26.7500
26.6700	26.6500	25.2000	25.1700
25.7400	25.7000	25.2500	25.7800
26.3500	26.6400	26.1500	25.8800
25.9400	25.7200	25.3700	25.1100
25.2600	25.7500	25.3200	25.5100
25.7800	26.1200	27.1000	27.5600
27.2000	27.4500	26.6000	26.2000
25.9100	26.2300	26.7400	27.8500
28.2000	28.5200	27.5000	26.6000
27.0900	27.8400	27.8600	

Data Test Sample Period : 1/6/67-12/21/67

Friday Weekly Observations for London and New York December Data

$[P_1^D(t)]$ [1] : N.Y. Dec. Cocoa Futures Low Price (U.S. ¢ Per Lb.):

25.5300	25.6500	26.5200	26.6500
26.8100	27.5000	27.5000	26.7000
26.3000	26.9000	27.1000	26.4000
26.3300	25.8000	24.9100	24.8800
25.6000	25.5900	25.1200	25.3500
26.1100	26.4600	25.8000	25.6400
25.8100	25.4900	24.7700	24.6600
24.8100	25.9400	25.1800	25.2100
25.6300	25.8800	26.6000	27.2000
27.3200	27.1500	26.4200	25.9700
25.4600	25.9500	26.3800	27.2000
27.8500	27.7200	26.9000	26.6000
26.9500	27.8000	27.8400	

Termination of December Data.

Friday Weekly Observations for U.K./U.S. Exchange Data

$t_s(t)$: U.K./U.S. Spot Exchange Rate:

279.010	279.050	279.100	279.260
279.530	279.470	279.420	279.260
279.430	279.580	279.640	279.770
279.750	279.880	280.040	279.890
279.880	279.890	279.720	279.540
279.460	279.280	279.260	279.200
278.960	279.000	278.920	278.860
278.660	278.600	278.530	278.450
278.590	278.430	278.560	278.390
278.350	278.310	278.360	278.340
278.250	278.300	278.290	278.240
278.260	278.250	242.000	242.000
240.750	240.090	240.500	

$t_3(t)$: U.K./U.S. 30 Day Forward Exchange Rate:

278.960	278.850	278.900	279.010
279.330	279.260	279.220	279.120
279.260	279.430	279.530	279.580
279.590	279.640	279.830	279.670
279.600	279.740	279.600	279.430
279.350	279.120	279.160	279.130
278.910	278.940	278.940	278.820
278.450	278.540	278.500	278.330
278.470	278.290	278.360	278.250
278.160	278.220	278.200	278.260
278.120	278.080	278.040	277.990
277.840	277.500	241.650	241.720
240.150	238.690	239.260	

Data Test Sample Period : 1/6/67-12/21/67

Friday Weekly Observations for U.K./U.S. Exchange Data

$t_6(t)$: U.K./U.S. 60 Day Forward Exchange Rate:

278.820	278.750	278.700	278.890
279.190	279.140	279.120	278.960
279.030	279.200	279.320	279.330
279.390	279.450	279.630	279.490
279.380	279.490	279.370	279.240
279.150	278.980	279.080	279.010
278.970	278.820	278.880	278.700
278.290	278.320	278.290	278.150
278.250	278.080	278.210	277.980
277.950	278.050	278.060	278.030
277.870	277.770	277.840	277.690
277.560	277.500	241.500	241.500
239.650	237.990	238.150	

$t_9(t)$: U.K./U.S. 90 Day Forward Exchange Rate:

278.620	278.570	278.620	278.760
278.990	278.930	278.920	278.750
278.890	279.030	279.160	279.170
279.210	279.260	279.430	279.290
279.200	279.350	279.200	279.050
278.990	278.840	278.940	278.890
278.680	278.700	278.740	278.630
278.140	278.170	278.140	278.010
278.130	277.930	278.050	277.810
277.800	277.830	277.920	277.880
277.710	277.640	277.640	277.490
277.340	276.900	241.300	241.300
239.250	237.390	237.550	

Termination of U.K./U.S. Exchange Data.

Data Test Sample Period : 1/6/67-9/22/67

Friday Weekly Observations for London and New York September Data

$P_2^S(t)$: London Sept. Cocoa Futures Price (U.K. Shillings Per Cwt):

212.000	211.600	219.000	221.600
223.600	231.600	232.000	224.000
220.000	223.600	226.600	224.000
223.000	223.600	211.600	212.000
213.600	211.600	208.000	211.600
214.000	217.600	214.600	213.000
213.000	211.000	207.600	207.000
207.000	209.000	209.000	210.000
212.600	215.000	220.000	226.000
226.000	225.600		

Data Test Sample Period : 1/6/67-9/22/67

Friday Weekly Observations for London and New York September Data

$[P_2^S(t)]_v$: London Sept. Cocoa Futures Price (U.S. ¢ Per Lb.)

U.K./U.S. Par Value Currency Conversion Rate:

26.5000	26.4500	27.3750	27.7000
27.9500	28.9500	29.0000	28.0000
27.5000	27.9500	28.3250	28.0000
27.8750	27.9500	26.4500	26.5000
26.7000	26.4500	26.0000	26.4500
26.7500	27.2000	26.8250	26.6250
26.6250	26.3750	25.9500	25.8750
25.8750	26.1250	26.1250	26.2500
26.5750	26.8750	27.5000	28.2500
28.2500	28.2000		

$[P_2^S(t)]_s$: London Sept. Cocoa Futures Price (U.S. ¢ Per Lb.)

U.K./U.S. Spot Currency Conversion Rate:

26.4063	26.3602	27.2870	27.6268
27.9030	28.8952	28.9399	27.9260
27.4440	27.9080	28.2885	27.9770
27.8501	27.9380	26.4538	26.4895
26.6885	26.4396	25.9740	26.4065
26.6984	27.1300	26.7541	26.5489
26.5261	26.2808	25.8499	25.7696
25.7511	25.9944	25.9878	26.1046
26.4411	26.7243	27.3585	28.0875
28.0835	28.0297		

$[P_2^S(t)]_3$

U.K./U.S. 30 Day Forward Currency Conversion Rate:

26.4015	26.3413	27.2674	27.6020
27.8831	28.8735	28.9192	27.9120
27.4273	27.8931	28.2774	27.9579
27.8341	27.9140	26.4339	26.4687
26.6618	26.4254	25.9628	26.3961
26.6879	27.1145	26.7445	26.5422
26.5213	26.2751	25.8517	25.7659
25.7317	25.9887	25.9850	26.0934
26.4297	26.7108	27.3389	28.0734
28.0643	28.0207		

Data Test Sample Period : 1/6/67-9/22/67

Friday Weekly Observations for London and New York September Data

$[P_2^S(t)]_6$: London Sept. Cocoa Futures Price (U.S. ¢ Per Lb.)

U.K./U.S. 60 Day Forward Currency Conversion Rate:

26.3883	26.3319	27.2479	27.5901
27.8691	28.8610	28.9088	27.8960
27.4047	27.8701	28.2562	27.9330
27.8142	27.8951	26.4150	26.4517
26.6408	26.4018	25.9415	26.3782
26.6687	27.1009	26.7368	26.5308
26.5270	26.2638	25.8462	25.7549
25.7169	25.9682	25.9654	26.0765
26.4089	26.6907	27.3242	28.0462
28.0431	28.0036		

$[P_2^S(t)]_9$: London Sept. Cocoa Futures Price (U.S. ¢ Per Lb.)

U.K./U.S. 90 Day Forward Currency Conversion Rate:

26.3694	26.3149	27.2400	27.5773
27.8492	28.8393	28.8881	27.8750
27.3909	27.8531	28.2400	27.9170
27.7963	27.8761	26.3961	26.4328
26.6237	26.3885	25.9257	26.3602
26.6535	27.0873	26.7234	26.5194
26.4995	26.2525	25.8332	25.7484
25.7031	25.9542	25.9514	26.0634
26.3975	26.6763	27.3085	28.0290
28.0280	27.9814		

$[A_{ij}^S(t)]_v^o$: Arbitrage Incentive Sept. Cocoa Futures (U.S. 0.01¢) Using

U.K./U.S. Par Value Currency Conversion Rate & N.Y. Opening Price:

1.40001	1.07002	0.775009	0.800003
0.700012	1.00002	1.20001	0.920013
1.25002	0.850006	1.16501	1.15002
1.37502	1.30002	1.70001	1.75002
1.25002	1.25000	1.26001	1.50002
0.800018	1.06001	1.10501	1.50502
1.27502	1.35501	1.15001	1.89502
1.37502	1.42500	1.66501	1.66002
1.67500	1.82501	1.00002	1.47002
1.85001	1.35002		

Data Test Sample Period : 1/6/67-9/22/67

Friday Weekly Observations for London and New York September Data

$[A^S_{ij}(t)]^o_s$: Arbitrage Incentive Sept. Cocoa Futures (U.S. 0.01¢) Using

U.K./U.S. Spot Currency Conversion Rate & N.Y. Opening Price:

1.30629	0.980255	0.686996	0.726761
0.653046	0.945175	1.13989	0.845978
1.19400	0.808029	1.12856	1.12700
1.35010	1.28799	1.70377	1.73956
1.23853	1.23956	1.23398	1.45651
0.748898	0.990036	1.03409	1.42894
1.17610	1.26080	1.04988	1.78963
1.25114	1.29436	1.52780	1.51466
1.54114	1.67429	0.858536	1.30754
1.68349	1.17976		

$[A^S_{ij}(t)]^l_s$: Arbitrage Incentive Sept. Cocoa Futures (U.S. 0.01¢) Using

U.K./U.S. Spot Currency Conversion Rate & N.Y. Low Price:

1.37628	1.01021	0.766998	0.846786
0.842987	1.01520	1.13988	1.02599
1.19400	1.04800	1.12848	1.47699
1.59007	2.12801	1.88379	1.96948
1.41847	1.25960	1.25400	1.50648
0.958389	1.01001	1.47409	1.42888
1.29607	1.38078	1.68987	1.80959
1.54108	1.34441	1.52777	1.65460
1.66109	1.87430	1.32846	1.36748
1.33348	1.47969		

$[A^S_{ij}(t)]^o_3$: Arbitrage Incentive Sept. Cocoa Futures (U.S. 0.01¢) Using

U.K./U.S. 30 Day Forward Currency Conversion Rate & N.Y. Opening Price:

1.30154	0.961349	0.667450	0.702026
0.633087	0.923477	1.11919	0.831970
1.17731	0.793076	1.11742	1.10797
1.33415	1.26404	1.68391	1.71875
1.21185	1.22540	1.22284	1.44614
0.737869	0.974487	1.02449	1.42226
1.17134	1.25513	1.05173	1.78593
1.23174	1.28873	1.52502	1.50340
1.52975	1.66086	0.838898	1.29343
1.66432	1.17072		

Data Test Sample Period : 1/6/67-9/22/67

Friday Weekly Observations for London and New York September Data

$[A_{ij}^S(t)]_6^o$: Arbitrage Incentive Sept. Cocoa Futures (U.S. 0.01¢) Using

U.K./U.S. 60 Day Forward Currency Conversion Rate & N.Y. Opening Price:

1.28828	0.951920	0.647903	0.690155
0.619125	0.911057	1.10883	0.815979
1.15472	0.770142	1.09618	1.08298
1.31424	1.24509	1.66502	1.70172
1.19086	1.20180	1.20146	1.42819
0.718765	0.960892	1.01685	1.41086
1.17705	1.24380	1.04617	1.77487
1.21696	1.26820	1.50543	1.48654
1.50888	1.64070	0.824173	1.26617
1.64314	1.15359		

$[A_{ij}^S(t)]_9^o$: Arbitrage Incentive Sept. Cocoa Futures (U.S. 0.01¢) Using

U.K./U.S. 90 Day Forward Currency Conversion Rate & N.Y. Opening Price:

1.26936	0.934891	0.640045	0.677307
0.599167	0.889343	1.08812	0.794983
1.14096	0.753159	1.08000	1.06699
1.29633	1.22612	1.64613	1.68279
1.17372	1.18855	1.18571	1.41025
0.703491	0.947281	1.00342	1.39943
1.14948	1.23254	1.03320	1.76837
1.20309	1.25423	1.49142	1.47343
1.49748	1.62630	0.808472	1.24901
1.62802	1.13142		

$[A_{ij}^S(t)]_9^h$

U.K./U.S. 90 Day Forward Currency Conversion Rate & N.Y. High Price:

0.619385	0.764893	0.440002	0.377258
0.569183	0.609268	0.748077	0.424988
0.490875	0.683075	0.900009	1.03700
1.16629	1.16608	1.47609	1.62280
1.16367	1.05847	1.13567	0.970200
0.663467	0.797272	1.00339	1.13939
1.09947	1.13249	1.03319	1.35840
1.07309	0.934189	1.32138	1.32339
1.46747	1.57628	0.918488	1.22899
1.07800	1.13139		

Data Test Sample Period : 1/6/67-9/22/67

Friday Weekly Observations for London and New York September Data

$[P_I^S(t)]^o$: N.Y. Sept. Cocoa Futures Opening Price (U.S. ¢ Per Lb.):

25.1000	25.3800	26.6000	26.9000
27.2500	27.9500	27.8000	27.0800
26.2500	27.1000	27.1600	26.8500
26.5000	26.6500	24.7500	24.7500
25.4500	25.2000	24.7400	24.9500
25.9500	26.1400	25.7200	25.1200
25.3500	25.0200	24.8000	23.9800
24.5000	24.7000	24.4600	24.5900
24.9000	25.0500	26.5000	26.7800
26.4000	26.8500		

$[P_I^S(t)]^h$: N.Y. Sept. Cocoa Futures High Price (U.S. ¢ Per Lb.):

25.7500	25.5500	26.8000	27.2000
27.2800	28.2300	28.1400	27.4500
26.9000	27.1700	27.3400	26.8800
26.6300	26.7100	24.9200	24.8100
25.4600	25.3300	24.7900	25.3900
25.9900	26.2900	25.7200	25.3800
25.4000	25.1200	24.8000	24.3900
24.6300	25.0200	24.6300	24.7400
24.9300	25.1000	26.3900	26.8000
26.9500	26.8500		

$[P_I^S(t)]^l$: N.Y. Sept. Cocoa Futures Low Price (U.S. ¢ Per Lb.):

25.0300	25.3500	26.5200	26.7800
27.0600	27.8800	27.8000	26.9000
26.2500	26.8600	27.1600	26.5000
26.2600	25.8100	24.5700	24.5200
25.2700	25.1800	24.7200	24.9000
25.7400	26.1200	25.2800	25.1200
25.2300	24.9000	24.1600	23.9600
24.2100	24.6500	24.4600	24.4500
24.7800	24.8500	26.0300	26.7200
26.7500	26.5500		

Termination of September Data.

Notes

Chapter 1

1. Chicago Mercantile Exchange, *Trading In Tomorrows,* pamphlet (Chicago: the author, 1969), p. 3.

2. Joseph R. Maxwell, *Facts and Factors for Commodity Futures Traders,* pamphlet (Chicago, Ill.: M–S Commodities, 1969), p. 2.

3. Hendrik S. Houthakker, "The Scope and Limits of Futures Tradings," in *The Allocation of Economic Resources: Essays in Honour of B. F. Haley,* ed. Moses Abramovitz and Armen Alchian et al. (Stanford, Cal.: Stanford University Press, 1959), pp. 134–59.

4. Belveal, L. Dee, ed., *Commodity Trading Manual,* commodity broker's manual (Chicago: Chicago Board of Trade, 1966), p. 3-a.

5. Ibid.

6. Holbrook Working, "Futures Trading and Hedging," *American Economic Review* 3 (June 1953): 314–43.

7. Because futures trading on organized commodity exchanges is conducted through legal detailed contract forms and adheres to strict trading rules, these markets are referred to as organized commodity markets. In contrast to futures, only a few spot markets are operated as organized markets.

8. Futures markets are distinct from other types of commodity markets in that "less than 3%" of all the contracts traded on an organized exchange are consummated by delivery. See Joseph R. Maxwell, *Facts and Factors for Commodity Futures Traders,* p. 1.

9. Jules I. Bogen and Samuel S. Shipman, eds. "Commodity Trading," in *Financial Handbook* (New York: Ronald Press Company, 1964), p. 23.1.

10. Ibid.

11. Ibid., p. 27.3.

12. The terms *straddle* and *spreading* are used in the cotton and grain trade respectively.

13. Robert L. Raclin, "Role of Markets in Determining Flow of Commodities in Domestic and International Trade," Discussion, Futures Trading Seminar, vol. 3, *A Commodity Marketing Forum for College Teachers of Economics* (Madison, Wis.: Mirmir Publishers, 1966), p. 211.

14. Gerald Gold, *Modern Commodity Futures Trading,* 4th ed. rev. (New York: Commodity Research Bureau, 140 Broadway, N.Y.), p. 229.

15. The trading hours for futures is comparatively short—from three to five hours, depending on the regulations of the exchanges. In most cases, metals futures have a shorter trading session.

16. On most British commodity exchanges, limits are not imposed on price movements. And in some U.S. exchanges, for example, The New York

Cocoa Exchange, there is no price limit on or after the first delivery month's notice day.

17. Technical factors may cause distorted interpretation of trading volume figures, as is true when heavy switching is taking place between different delivery months.

18. Bogen and Shipman, "Commodity Trading," pp. 23, 29.

19. Ibid., p. 23.3.

20. *Investor's Reader,* "Commodity Trading Booms in Year of Quieter Stock Activity," 10:53, (November 19, 1969): 16–17.

21. Switching consists of two separate transactions. One is the sale of a nearby delivery contract month and the simultaneous purchase of a more distant future, or vice versa. Switching is used to maintain an active position in commodity futures for either hedging or speculative purposes.

22. As previously mentioned, there are certain substitutable grades and alternative discount and premium grades that are tenderable.

23. Bogen and Shipman, "Commodity Trading," p. 23.4.

24. Ibid., p. 23.6.

25. One notable exception is the future metals traded on the London exchange, which designates "forward" deliveries as foreign currency exchanges do. Copper, lead, zinc, and tin futures are sold forward with the deferred delivery taking place in either 30 or 60 days depending on the contract's specifications. Each commodity exchange has its specific unit of trading that is equivalent to the quality of the commodity covered by the futures contract.

26. Bogen and Shipman, "Commodity Trading," p. 23.17.

27. The regulation of margin deposits that has been adopted by all U.S. futures exchanges is that initial margins on speculative accounts carried by brokerage firms will be smaller than those of clearing members of an exchange.

28. The clearinghouse is sometimes referred to as the Clearing Association; it is an agency established for each futures exchange, through which all transactions by exchange members must be financially settled.

29. F. Helmut Weymar, *The Dynamics of the World Cocoa Market* (Cambridge, Mass.: M.I.T. Press, 1968), p. 6.

30. Ibid., pp. 5, 7.

31. The sole exception is after the first notice for the spot month, when no limits are established.

Chapter 2

1. Karl Menger, "On the Origins of Money," trans. Caroline Foley, *Economics Journal* 2 (1892): 248.

2. For earlier impressive works on the temporal and spatial economics

of closely related markets for the same commodity, see Roger W. Gray, "The Relationship Among Three Futures Markets: An Importance of Speculation," *Food Research Institute Studies* 1 (February 1961): 21–32; M. H. Peston and B. S. Yamey, "Inter-temporal Price Relationships with Forward Markets: A Method of Analysis," *Economics* 108 (November 1960): 355–67.

3. For an interesting discussion on history and working of arbitrage in security markets, see Meyers H. Weinstein, *Arbitrage in Securities* (New York: Harper & Bros., 1931).

4. *Wool,* Commodity Report (New York: Merrill Lynch, May 1966), p. 41.

5. Mary Saint Albang and Roy Stevens, *Sugar,* Hawaiian Sugar Planters' Association, Commodity Report (New York: Merrill Lynch, 1968), pp. 42–43.

6. *Wool,* pp. 41–42.

7. With the exception of the Merrill Lynch Sugar Study, *Cocoa,* Commodity Report published by Merrill Lynch, New York, August 1966, p. 54, the others are studies that were conducted prior to the 1967 sterling devaluation. This may serve to indicate that arbitrage must have made its presence known during the 1949 devaluation of the pound. Its presence, unfortunately, cannot be examined empirically because of data insufficiency.

8. Paul A. Samuelson, "The Dynamics of Speculation and Risk," chap. 22 in *Economics, An Introductory Analysis,* 2d ed., (New York: McGraw-Hill Book Co., 1951) p. 442.

9. Although the above discussion centers on spatial arbitrage, it could easily lend itself to temporal arbitrage as well. This is tenable because economic relations in *time* have many of the properties of economic relations in *space*.

10. The algebraic notation and diagramatic representation developed in this section borrow heavily from Professor Samuelson's pioneering articles: Paul A. Samuelson, "Spatial Price Equilibrium and Linear Programming, *American Economic Review* (June 1952), also published in *The Collected Scientific Papers of Paul A. Samuelson,* vol. 2, ed. Joseph E. Stiglitz (Cambridge, Mass.: M.I.T. Press, 1966): 925–45; and Paul A. Samuelson, "Intertemporal Price Equilibrium: A Prologue to the Theory of Speculation," (*Weltwirtschaftliches Archiv,* December 1957), also published in *The Collected Scientific Papers of Paul A. Samuelson,* vol. 2, pp. 946–84.

11. In the empirical section of this study, the superscript will be occasionally replaced by the letters S for September and D for December, rather than the numerical values shown in the parenthetical expression $f = (1, 2, 3, \ldots, n)$. This is intended to prevent any confusion that might arise from observing a futures contract at different points in time.

12. Samuelson, "Intertemporal Price Equilibrium," p. 948.

13. *Note*: The London price is treated as though it had been converted

by means of the existing exchange rate to the New York unit of account. The same would be true for physical unit weights between futures contracts.

14. This discussion is indebted to Paul A. Samuelson's celebrated paper, "Proof that Properly Anticipated Prices Fluctuate Randomly," *Industrial Management Review* 6 (Spring 1965): 41–49.

15. The term *basis* is to be treated synonymously with the term *spread* throughout the development of this study.

16. The intertemporal analysis developed in this chapter assumes two simultaneous but opposite positions at both periods of the arbitrage. If an arbitrageur is long in futures at the initial trading period t, he is also, it is assumed, automatically short in spot or vice versa. The same assumption is made regarding the terminal trading period, $t + k$. The argument also develops itself around the spot futures relation that assumes that arbitrageurs are willing to carry positive or negative inventories. However, this assumption can easily be avoided by substituting the spread relation between futures instead of the spot-futures relation.

17. This assumes that random disturbances have caused a momentary inconsistency between the spot and futures expected values. Also, the equality and inequality statements are intended to connote increases or decreases over time that under conditions of perfect foresight would be associated with certainty values.

18. In American parlance, *positive carrying charges* and *inverse carrying charges* refer to the British equivalents of *contango* and *normal backwardation* respectively.

Chapter 3

1. This topic has rarely been referred to in the literature. This neglect might be partially explained by Paul Cootner's observation that "many academicians find discussions of future and hedging hard to follow." See Paul H. Cootner, "Speculation and Hedging," *Food Research Institute Studies* (Special issue, 1965), pp. 65–103. For earlier studies that probe the issue of the interrelationships between foreign exchange depreciation and commodity markets, the reader is directed to Li Choh-Ming, "The Effects of Depreciated Exchange Upon Merchandise Movements," *Quarterly Journal of Economics* 49 (May 1935): 495–502; William Aneurin, "A Fixed Value of Bullion Standard: A Proposal for Preventing General Fluctuations of Trade," *Economic Journal* 2 (June 1892): 280–89; F. W. Taussig, "Silver Situation, The International," *Quarterly Journal of Economics* 11 (October 1896): 1–35; and J. M. Clark, "Possible Complications of the Compensated Dollar," *American Economic Review* 3 (September 1913): 576–88.

2. In the concluding chapter, the arbitrage incentive is traced during sterling crisis periods in which devaluation was not enacted.

3. The phrase *structure of the test sample* indicates an odd peculiarity,

it shows a combination of inverse and positive carrying charge between delivery periods. The spot price is greater than the nearest future. However, instead of price discounting continuing among the contracts that followed, the maturity structure began to take a premium inclination with the most distant futures approaching the time path of the spot price. A similar situation was encountered in an econometric examination of the term structure of foreign exchange rates; see John R. Dominguez, "An Empirical Investigation of the Relationship between Speculation and Price Stability in a Floating Foreign Exchange Market," *Amercian Economist* 1 (Spring 1971): 3–20. An earlier version of this paper was presented at the 1970 Detroit meetings of the American Economic Association.

4. The New York closing price was eliminated from consideration because it takes place at a time when the London Cocoa Terminal has closed its trading session and thus cancels out the possibility of simultaneous arbitrage.

5. One of the interesting outcomes that resulted from trying to select the appropriate representative price was the negligible difference between the opening and the midpoint prices throughout the test sample.

6. *Cocoa,* Commodity Report (New York: Merrill Lynch, August 1966), p. 53.

7. Three observations of the opening price were outside the high and low price ranges. The reason for this situation is that heavy transaction pressures may drive the opening beyond the high-to-low price range. Typically high and low prices are recorded after the opening of the trading session.

8. *Cocoa,* August 1966, p. 54.

9. Only in three instances was the term structure of sterling's rate of foreign exchange $\pounds_2(t) > \pounds_3(t) > \pounds_6(t) > \pounds_9(t)$ disturbed. When the above inequality was altered, this situation rarely resulted in one exchange rate's exceeding the nearest forward rate by more than one hundredth of a cent. Still, it did have enough impact to affect significantly the London–New York futures price differential.

10. Paul Einzig, *A Dynamic Theory of Forward Exchange* (New York: Macmillan & Co., St. Martin's Press, 1961), p. 120.

11. "The Foreign Exchange Market in Great Britain," chap. 11, in *The International Market for Foreign Exchange,* ed. Robert Z. Aliber (New York: Praeger Special Studies in International Economics and Development, 1969), pp. 89–90. The reader is also encouraged to direct his attention to the other excellent contributions presented in Aliber, ed., *International Market*, especially Oscar L. Altman, "Eurodollar and Foreign Exchange Markets," pp. 20–29; Alexander Swoboda, "Vehicle Currencies and the Foreign Exchange Market: The Case of the Dollar," pp. 30–40; Helmut Lipfert, "Psychology of the Exchange Market," pp. 123–36, and "Measures to Improve the Depth, Breadth, and Resiliency of the Exchange Markets," pp. 235–42; John Spraos, "Some Aspects of Sterling in the

Decade 1957–66," pp. 158–74; Robert A. Mundell, "The Cost of Exchange Crises and the Problem of Sterling," pp. 209–21; and Robert Z. Aliber, "Central Bank Intervention in the Foreign Exchange Market," pp. 222–34.

12. Aliber, "Foreign Exchange Market in Great Britain," p. 90.

13. *Cocoa,* August, 1966, p. 54.

14. Mary Saint Albang and Roy Stevens, *Sugar,* Hawaiian Sugar Planters' Association, Commodity Report (New York: Merrill Lynch, 1968), p. 42.

15. A similar concept was developed earlier by Aliber in his study "Speculation in Foreign Exchanges: The European Experience 1919–1926," *Yale Economic Essays* 2 (Spring 1962): 171–245.

16. Ibid., p. 176.

17. For a well-detailed discussion of alternative corrective measures, see Fritz Machlup, *On Terms, Concepts, Theories and Strategies in the Discussion of Greater Flexibility of Exchange Rates,* Reprints in International Finance 14, Princeton, N.J. [Reprinted from *Banca Nazionale del Lavoro Quarterly Review* 92 (March 1970)].

18. Fred Hirsch, *The Pound Sterling: A Polemic* (London: Victor Gollancz, 1965), p. 16.

19. *Economist,* "Would you have done better in futures?" vol. 7, June 1971, p. 86.

20. Joseph A. Walpole, *New Guide to Successful Commodity Speculation* (Newton Center, Mass.: Library of Wall Street, 1966), p. 22.

21. *Note*: The diagrams discussed have been modified to include daily observations within the weekly interval of a given month. This was necessary alteration, in order to single out certain events that might be considered to have a significant impact on devaluation expectations. The time unit used in the illustrations divides the observation period as follows: The largest vertical bars represent the terminating Friday observation for that given month. They serve to separate the weekly trading periods between the various months. The intermediate size bars designate Friday weekly observations also, except they do not divide the monthly periods and are instead, observations within a month. The smallest vertical bars indicate specific daily observation.

22. Paul A. Samuelson, "Intertemporal Price Equilibrium: A Prologue to the Theory of Speculation," *Weltwirtschaftliches Archiv* 2. (December 1957): 948. Also published in *The Collected Scientific Papers of Paul A. Samuelson,* vol. 2, ed. Joseph E. Stiglitz. (Cambridge, Mass.: M.I.T. Press, 1966), pp. 946–84.

23. *The Devaluation of the Pound,* Special Research Report (Cambridge, Mass.: Northern Research and Engineering Corp., November 1967), p. 27.

24. *Market Letter,* Commodity Research Report, Rittenhouse Investments, Inc. August 15, 1969, p. 6.

25. *As We See It,* Commodity Firm Newsletter, B. J. Lind & Co., August 14, 1969, p. 2; ibid., August 21, 1969, p. 2.

Chapter 4

1. The sterling crisis peak periods examined are historically similar to those cited by John Spraos in his Ditchley Park conference paper, "Some Aspects of Sterling in the Decade 1957–66," in *The International Market for Foreign Exchange,* ed. R. Z. Aliber (New York: Praeger, 1969), pp. 158–76.

2. Fred Hirsch, *The Pound Sterling: A Polemic* (London: Victor Gollancz, 1965), p. 49.

3. The assumption in this case is that the 75–100-point spread is the appropriate equilibrium basis range for the year 1957.

4. "U.K. Spur to Competition Looms," *Journal of Commerce,* July 12, 1961, p. 13.

5. Under normal circumstances, we should not expect a negative price differential between London and New York, i.e., $P_2(t) - P_1(t) < 0$. To check against possible errors in the data, several other published sources were used as a cross check, and it was found that there were no recorded data inconsistencies.

6. "World Money Front," *Journal of Commerce,* May 29, 1961, p. 9.

7. Ibid., June 19, 1961, p. 19.

8. Ibid., July 10, 1961, p. 11.

9. Ibid., July 25, 1961, p. 23.

10. Ibid., July 26, 1961, p. 23.

11. "Commodity Futures," *Journal of Commerce,* July 26, 1961, p. 8.

12. "World Money Front," *Journal of Commerce,* September 8, 1961, p. 23.

13. "From Trader's Wires British Reserves," *Journal of Commerce,* September 8, 1964, p. 23.

14. "Bid for More Exports and Higher Money Rates Foreseen for Britain," *Journal of Commerce,* October 19, 1964, p. 11.

15. Hirsch, *The Pound Sterling,* pp. 57–58.

16. Ibid., pp. 83–84.

17. "World Money Front," *Journal of Commerce,* July 25, 1966, p. 23.

18. Ibid., August 15, 1966, p. 25.

19. Ibid., September 16, 1966, p. 21.

20. A number of studies have been conducted to determine the term structure of interest rates; some of these are J. M. Culbertson, "Term Structure of Interest Rates," *Quarterly Journal of Economics* 71 (November 1957): 485–517; R. A. Kessel, *The Cyclical Behavior of the Term Structure of Interest Rates,* Occasional Paper 91 (New York: National Bureau of Economic Research, 1965); F. Lutz, "The Structure of Interest Rates," *Quarterly Journal of Economics* 60 (February 1940): 36–63; B. G. Malkiel, "Expectations, Bond Prices and the Term Structure of Interest

Rates," *Quarterly Journal of Economics* 76 (May 1962): 197–218; D. Meiselman, *The Term Structure of Interest Rates* (Prentice-Hall: Englewood Cliffs, N.J.: 1962); and F. Modigliani and R. Sutch, "Innovations in Interest Rate Policy," *American Economic Review* 56 (May 1966): 178–97.

Glossary

Arbitrageur   Person who buys and sells in accordance with price differences between commodities and markets over time.

Ask price   In security or futures trading, the price at which a seller of a stock or commodity is willing to sell.

Basis, or Contract grades   Grades of a commodity that are eligible for delivery on a futures contract.

Basis equilibrium   See **Spread.**

Bear   One who expects prices to decline.

Call   Exchange practice that notifies traders that a trading session for a specific delivery month is about to begin. The call procedure establishes opening prices for all delivery months in a systematic manner.

Carrying charge   Cost of carrying a commodity in storage over a period of time, usually including warehouse and interest charges, insurance, and so forth.

Clearinghouse   Agency, established for each futures exchange, through which all transactions by exchange members must be cleared.

Close   Period at end of trading session. Also, price, or range of prices that prevail at this time, determined by those transactions officially declared to have been made at the close.

Closing gong   Signal indicating that no more trading can take place that day.

Commodity exchange   Association of traders that provides an organized market for the purchase and sale of certain commodities. Although futures contracts are signed at the exchange, the commodities are not delivered until a later period specified by the contract.

Contango   See **Positive carrying charges.**

Contract grade   See **Basis.**

Cover   To buy in or close out a short position.

Daily price variation limit   See **Maximum daily limit.**

Delivery month   Month during which the sold commodity must be delivered, as dictated by the futures contract.

Delivery points   Permanent sites designated officially by the various commodity exchanges for the delivery of specific commodities. In accordance with the type of commodity contract, there may be more than one delivery point.

Dynamic (two-period) arbitrage   Initial and terminal periods of an arbitrage transaction are separated by a time interval, so that price and spread movements must be considered over time rather than at a single moment in time.

Equilibrium basis range   Range in which the equilibrium basis fluctuates because of random disturbances; also, the upper and lower bounds for the price differential between London and New York.

Fair letter In the Middle Ages, the merchant's promissory contract assuring the buyer of future delivery of the purchased commodity; precursor of the current bill of exchange.

Fixed price differential Differences in price between the grades of a commodity as fixed by the contract's terms.

Forward exchange Contract for future delivery of foreign currency whose maturities are usually for periods 30, 60, and 90 days; often referred to as forward rates.

Futures Contracts to buy and receive or to sell and deliver a commodity during a specified future month; the terms of such contracts are standardized by the futures exchanges on which they are traded.

Hedge A sale of futures against an equivalent holding of an actual commodity, or vice versa, the purpose of which is to protect the hedger against adverse effects of price movements on his previous commitments; an offsetting transaction.

High Highest price at which a commodity is sold during the market day.

Inverse carrying charges The market is described as inverted when the spot price is greater than the futures price, or when the futures price for near months is greater than the futures price for distant months.

Long Term descriptive of trader who is holding a commodity, or whose net sum for purchases exceeds the amount of his sales. Also, the purchase of a futures contract.

Low Lowest price at which a commodity is sold during the market day.

Margin Cash deposit required of both buyers and sellers of futures by brokerage firms and clearinghouses, to ensure the fulfillment of contract commitments. There are two types of margins—initial, or original, and maintenance.

Maximum daily limit Maximum amount prices may vary in one trading session, in either direction, from the closing price of the previous day. The limit is determined by each exchange.

Minimum fluctuation Rule imposed by each exchange to restrict single price movement in a trading session to a set fractional amount.

Normal backwardation See **Inverse carrying charges.**

Open interest The number of futures contracts recorded in the clearinghouse books as "open" on the clearing brokers' books at the close of the market each day.

Opening Period at the beginning of the trading session. Also, the price of a commodity, or range of prices, that prevails at this time and is determined by those transactions officially declared to have been made at the opening.

Parity rate   Official exchange rate between the currencies of two countries that makes the purchasing power of one currency equivalent to that of the other.

Pits   Designated spaces on the exchange floor at which futures trading for particular commodities takes place.

Positive carrying charges   A market is described as showing positive carrying charges when the spot price is less than the futures price, or when the futures price for the nearest months is less than the futures price for distant months.

Rings   See **Pits**.

Seller's option   Right of seller to select, within limits of the contract, the grade of commodity, and the time and place of delivery.

Shoguns   A well-to-do Japanese feudal class, who, toward the end of the seventeenth century, issued receipts, the predecessors of futures, against rice being grown in the fields.

Short   A trader is described as short when the net sum of his sales exceeds the amount of his purchases. Also, the sale of a futures contract.

Spot market (or Cash market)   Market in which contracts are intended to be fulfilled immediately.

Spot rate   Current market exchange rate between currencies.

Spread   The difference between prices for the same or different commodities for two delivery months in the same or different markets. Also, the purchase of one future against the sale of another in order to profit from such a price difference. *Spread* is typically used in reference to grain, while *straddle* is used for other commodities.

Static (one-period) arbitrage   Condition existing when the initial and terminal periods of an arbitrage transaction and all adjustments are assumed to take place instantaneously.

Straddle   See **Spread**.

Switching   Sale of a near (delivery contract month) future, and the simultaneous purchase of a distant future, or vice versa.

Tender   To deliver a commodity in fulfillment of a futures contract.

Trading volume   Total amount of transactions completed in a trading session. Daily volume figures are published by all commodity exchanges to indicate the market breadth for that commodity.

Variable price differential   Price differences between the grades of a commodity determined on the basis of average commercial differentials prevailing from day to day in bona fide spot markets.

Bibliography

Aliber, R. Z. "Central Bank Intervention in the Foreign Exchange Market." In *The International Market for Foreign Exchange*, pp. 222–34. New York: Praeger Special Studies in International Economics and Development, 1969.

———. "Speculation in Foreign Exchanges: The European Experience 1919–1926." *Yale Economic Essays* (Spring 1962), pp. 171–245.

Aliber, R. Z., ed. *The International Market for Foreign Exchange*. New York: Praeger, 1969.

Altman, Oscar L. "Eurodollar and Foreign Exchange Markets." In *The International Market for Foreign Exchange*, pp. 20–29. New York: Praeger, 1969.

Bogen, Jules I. and Samuel S. Shipman, eds. "Commodity Trading." In *Financial Handbook*, pp. 23.1–23.35. New York: Ronald Press Company, 1964.

Branson, William. "The Minimum Covered Interest Differential Needed for International Arbitrage Activity." *Journal of Political Economy* (November) December 1969, pp. 1028–35.

Clark, J. M. "Possible Complications of the Compensated Dollar. *American Economic Review* (September 1913), pp. 576–88.

Cootner, Paul H. "Speculation and Hedging." *Food Research Institute Studies*, (Special issue) 1968, pp. 65–103.

Dominguez, John R. "An Empirical Investigation of the Relationship between Speculation and Price Stability in a Floating Foreign Exchange Market." *American Economist* (Spring 1971), pp. 3–20.

Einzig, Paul. *A Dynamic Theory of Forward Exchange*. New York: Macmillan and Co., St. Martin's Press.

Gold, Gerald. *Modern Commodity Futures Trading*, 4th ed. rev. New York: Commodity Research Bureau, 1966.

Gray, Roger W. "The Relationship Among Three Futures Markets: An Importance of Speculation." Food Research Institute Studies, (February 1961), pp. 21–32.

Hirsch, Fred. *The Pound Sterling: A Polemic*. London: Victor Gollancz, 1965.

Houthakker, Hendrik S. "The Scope and Limits of Futures Trading." In *The Allocation of Economic Resources: Essays in Honour of B. F. Haley*, edited by Moses Abramovitz and Armen Alchian et al., pp. 134–59. Stanford, Cal.: Stanford University Press, 1959.

Kessel, R. A. *"The Cyclical Behavior of the Term Structure of Interest Rates."* Occasional Paper 91. New York: National Bureau of Economic Research, 1965.

Li, Chol-Ming. "The Effect of Depreciated Exchange upon Merchandise Movements." *Quarterly Journal of Economics* 49 (May 1935): 495–502.

Lipfert, Helmut. "Measures to Improve the Depth, Breadth, and Resiliency of the Exchange Markets." In *The International Market for Foreign Exchange*, pp. 235–42. New York: Praeger, 1969.

———. "Psychology of the Exchange Market." In *The International Market for Foreign Exchange*, pp. 123–36. New York: Praeger, 1969.

Lutz, F. "The Structure of Interest Rates." *Quarterly Journal of Economics*, no. 60 (February 1940), pp. 36–63.

Machlup, F. *On Terms, Concepts, Theories and Strategies in the Discussion of Greater Flexibility of Exchange Rates*. Reprints in International Finance 14,

Princeton, N.J. [Reprinted from *Banca Nazionale del Lavoro Quarterly, Review*, no. 92 (March 1970)].

Malkiel, B. G. "Expectation Bond Prices and the Term Structure of Interest Rates." *Quarterly Journal of Economics*, no. 76 (May 1962), pp. 197–218.

Meiselman, D. *The Term Structure of Interest Rates.* Englewood Cliffs, N.J.: Prentice-Hall, 1962.

Menger, K. "On the Origin of Money." Translated by Caroline A Foley. *Economic Journal*, no. 2 (1892), pp. 239–35.

Modigliani, F. and R. Sutch. "Innovations in Interest Rate Policy." *American Economic Review*, no. 56 (May 1966), pp. 178–97.

Mundell, R. A. "The Cost of Exchange Crises and the Problem of Sterling." In *The International Market for Foreign Exchange*, pp. 209–21. New York: Praeger, 1969.

Peston, M. H. and B. S. Yamey. "Inter-Temporal Price Relationship with Forward Markets: A Method of Analysis." *Economica*, no. 108 (November 1960), pp. 355–67.

Raclin, R. L. "Role of Markets in Determining Flow of Commodities in Domestic and International Trade," (discussion) Futures Trading Seminar. Vol. 3, *A Commodity Marketing Forum for College Teachers of Economics.* Madison, Wisconsin: Mirmir Publishers, 1966. Pp. 206–21.

Samuelson, Paul A. "Intertemporal Price Equilibrium: A Prologue to the Theory of Speculation." (*Weltwirtschaftliches Archiv*, December 1957). In *The Collected Scientific Papers of Paul A. Samuelson*, vol. 2, edited by Joseph E. Stiglitz, pp. 946–84, Cambridge, Mass.: M.I.T. Press, 1966.

———. "Spatial Price Equilibrium and Linear Programming." (*American Economic Review*, June 1952). In *The Collected Scientific Papers of Paul A. Samuelson*, vol. 2, edited by Joseph E. Stiglitz, pp. 295–945. Cambridge, Mass.: M.I.T. Press, 1966.

———. "The Dynamics of Speculation and Risk." Chapter 22, *Economics, An Introductory Analysis*, 2d ed., p. 462. New York: McGraw-Hill Book Co., 1951.

———. "Proof that Properly Anticipated Prices Fluctuate Randomly." *Industrial Management Review*, no. 6 (Spring 1965), pp. 41–49.

Spraos, J. "Some Aspects of Sterling in the Decade 1957–1966." *The International Market for Foreign Exchange.* New York: Praeger, 1969, pp. 158–76.

Stiglitz, J. E., ed. *The Collected Scientific Papers of Paul A. Samuelson*, vol. 2. Cambridge, Mass.: M.I.T. Press, 1966.

Swoboda, A. "Vehicle Currencies and the Foreign Exchange Market: The Case of the Dollar," *The International Market for Foreign Exchange*, pp. 30–40. New York: Praeger, 1969.

Taussig, F. W. "Silver Situation, The International." *Quarterly Journal of Economics*, no. 11 (October 1896), pp. 1–35.

Weinstein, Meyer H. *Arbitrage in Securities.* New York: Harper & Bros., 1931.

Weymar, F. H. *The Dynamics of the World Cocoa Market.* Cambridge, Mass.: M.I.T. Press, 1968.

Williams, A. "A 'Fixed Value of Bullion' Standard: A Proposal for Preventing General Fluctuations of Trade." *Economic Journal* 2 (June 1892): 280–89.

Working, H. "Futures Trading and Hedging." *American Economic Review*, no. 3 (June 1953), pp. 314–43.

Special Periodical Publications

Albang, Mary Saint and Roy Stevens. *Sugar,* Hawaiian Sugar Planters Association Commodity Report published by Merrill Lynch, New York 1968.

As We See It, B.J. Lind & Company Commodity Newsletter (August 14, 1969).

As We See It, B.J. Lind & Company Commodity Newsletter (August 21, 1969).

Belveal, L. Dee, ed., *Commodity Trading Manual,* Commodity Brokers Manual, Chicago Board of Trade, 1966.

Cocoa, Commodity Report, Merrill Lynch, New York, August 1966.

"Commodity Trading Booms in Year of Quieter Stock Activity," *Investor's Reader,* Merrill Lynch 10 (November 19, 1969) pp. 16–17.

The Devaluation of the Pound, Special Research Report Northern Research and Engineering Corporation, Cambridge, Mass., November 1967.

Holmes, Alan and Francis Schott. *The New York Foreign Exchange Market,* Monograph Federal Reserve Bank of New York, February 1965.

Journal of Commerce, "Bid for More Exports, and Higher Money Rates Foreseen for Britain, October 19, 1964, pp. 1, 3, 11.

———, "Commodity Futures" July 26, 1961, p. 8.

———, "From Trader's Wires British Reserves," September 8, 1964, p. 23.

———, "U.K. Spur to Competition Looms," July 12, 1961, p. 13.

———, "World Money Front," July 25, 1966, p. 23.

———, "World Money Front," August 15, 1966, p. 25.

———, "World Money Front," September 16, 1966, p. 21.

———, "World Money Front," May 29, 1961, p. 9.

———, "World Money Front," June 19, 1961, p. 19.

———, "World Money Front," July 10, 1961, p. 11.

———, "World Money Front," July 25, 1961, p. 23.

———, "World Money Front," July 26, 1961, p. 23.

———, "World Money Front," September 8, 1961, p. 23.

Market Letter, Rittenhouse Investments, Inc., August 15, 1969.

Maxwell, Joseph R., *Facts and Factors for Commodity Futures Traders,* pamphlet published by M–S Commodities Inc., Illinois, 1969.

Trading in Tomorrows, pamphlet, Chicago Mercantile Exchange, 1969.

Wall Street Journal, "British Goods' Price May Not Fall as Fast or Far as Expected," November 21, 1967, p. 7.

Walpole, Joseph A., *New Guide to Successful Commodity Speculation,* Library of Wall Street, 1966.

Wool, Commodity Report, Merrill Lynch, New York, May 1966.

"Would You Have Done Better in Futures?" *Economist* 231 (June 7, 1969): 86–91.

Index

Albang, Mary Saint, 90
Aliber, Robert Z., 49, 90-91
Altman, Oscar L., 90
Aneurin, William, 88
Arbitrage:
    Incentive, 17
    Interspatial, 13
    Intertemporal, 13
    One-Period (Static) Under Certainty, 16, 18-21
    One-Period (Static) Under Uncertainty, 16, 31-33
    Two-Period (Dynamic) Under Certainty, 16-17, 21-31
    Two-Period (Dynamic) Under Uncertainty, 16-17, 34-35
Arbitrageurs, 4, 13
Association of Commodity Exchange Firms, Inc., 5

Bank of England, 37, 77, 80
Basis:
    Equilibrium, 23-29, 32, 46-77
    Equilibrium range, 65-73
    Joint market equilibrium, 32
    Spot futures, 17, 22-29, 44
Basis as "Contract Grade," 7, 10
Belveal, L. Dee, 1, 85
Bogen, Jules I., 2-8, 85-86
British Council on Price & Productivity, 71

Cagan, Philip, 55
Carrying charges:
    Allowance, 22
    Inverse, 16, 22-23, 30
    Positive, 16, 22-23, 32
Clark, John M., 88
Cocoa, 9-11, 14-15, 18-21, 29-32
Commodity grading, 7
Commodity markets, cash or spot, 2-3
Conservative Party, 66
Contract maturities, 13
Cootner, Paul H., 88
Culbertson, John M., 91

Devaluation, 15, 37-77
Dominguez, John R., 89
Differential:
    Fixed, 7
    Variable, 7-8

Einzig, Paul, 49, 89

"Fair Letter," 1

Finance Bill of 1961, 71
Food & Agricultural Organization of the UN, 10
Foreign Exchange Rates:
    Forward, 51, 65-66, 73
    Parity, 62, 66, 73
    Spot, 50, 80
Forward or "to arrive":
    Delivery, 2
    Sales, 10
Futures:
    Contracts, 6-11, 31
    Markets, 2, 13, 45
    Trading, 8, 15-16, 18

Ghana Cocoa Marketing Board, 10
Gill and Duffus, Ltd., 10
Gold, Gerald, 4, 85
Gray, Roger W., 87

Hedgers, hedging, 3, 13, 30, 54
Hirsch, Fred, 56, 66, 77, 90-91
Holmes, Oliver Wendell, 6
Houthakker, Hendrik S., 1, 85

International Monetary Fund, 71, 74
Interspatial price effects, 37, 57-79
Intertemporal price effects, 51-79

Kessel, Reuben A., 91

Labor Party, 37, 73
Leverage, financial, 46
Lipfert, Helmut, 89
Lloyd, Selwyn, 71
Lutz, Friedrich A., 91

Machlup, Fritz, 90
Malkiel, Burton G., 91
Margins:
    Futures, 8-9
    Stock, 8-9
Maxwell, Joseph R., 1, 85
Meiselman, David, 92
Menger, Karl, 13, 86
Merrill, Lynch, Pierce, Fenner & Smith, Inc., 15, 47
Ming, Li-Choh, 88
Modigliani, Franco, 92
Mundell, Robert A., 90

"Offsetting transaction," 6
"Open outcry," 4

Peston, M.H., 87
Price:
　Daily variation limit, 4
　Futures, 4, 15–17, 21–32, 43–46
　Minimum variation, 11
　Spot or "cash," 13–17, 21–23, 44

Raclin, Robert L., 4, 85
"Rings" or "Pits," 2

Samuelson, Paul A., 8, 18, 20, 64, 87–88, 90
"Scalpers," 3
Shipman, Samuel S., 2–8, 85–86
Shoguns, 1
Spraos, John, 89, 91
Spread:
　Actual, 15–17, 21–36, 46–64, 66, 71
　Discounted, 46, 71, 74
　Equilibrium, 15–36, 46–64

Premium, 29, 37, 45–46
Stevens, Roy, 51, 90
Stiglitz, Joseph E., 87, 90
"Straddle," 5, 14, 22, 34
"Straddler," 4
Sutch, Richard, 92
"Switching," 6
Swoboda, Alexander, 89

Taussig, F.W., 88

Walpole, Joseph A., 57, 90
Weinstein, Meyer H., 87
Weymar, F. Helmut, 9, 86
Working, Holbrook, 1, 85
World Monetary Front, 72–3, 80

Yamey, B.S., 87

About the Author

John R. Dominguez was born in 1937 in San Bernardino, California. He received his B.A. Degree in Economics from the University of Southern California in June, 1968. Graduating with honors, he is also a Phi Beta Kappa and Woodrow Wilson Fellow. He received the Ph.D. Degree in economics from the Massachusetts Institute of Technology, in June 1971.

Dr. Dominguez is now Assistant Professor of Business Economics and Finance in the Graduate School of Management at the University of California at Los Angeles. Formerly, he was Visiting Professor in the Business School at Boston University, 1970–71 Academic Year, Lecturer at I.A.C.E. (the Instituto de Administracion Cientifica de las Empresas, Mexico City, Mexico), Consultant to the Governor's Advisory Council of Puerto Rico, and Economic Consultant in the Bureau of Education and Cultural Affairs in the U.S. State Department.

His publications include: *Journal articles;* "A Theory of Economic Growth and Inflation," "Comment," *American Economist,* Vol. XII:1 (Spring, 1968), "An Empirical Investigation on the Relationship Between Speculation and Price Stability in a Floating Foreign Exchange Market," *American Economist,* Vol. XIV:1 (Spring, 1971), "An Analysis of the Industrial Relations System in a Collective Society," *British Journal of Industrial Relations,* Vol. IX:1 (March, 1971).

Dr. Dominguez is currently heading a Ford Foundation and U.C.L.A. study of banking and capital flows in minority areas which focuses on Mexican-American community centers.

He is also presently the Director of the U.C.L.A.-I.A.C.E. Executive Program. This is an advanced management program jointly sponsored by the U.C.L.A. faculty and the Instituto de Administracion Cientifica de las Empresas (I.A.C.E.) which is designed to develop management skills and relate them to the Mexican executives' needs and culture.